LOUD
and CLEAR

LOUD and CLEAR

A Guide to Effective Communication

SY LAZARUS

Cartoons by Henry Martin

amacom

A DIVISION OF AMERICAN MANAGEMENT ASSOCIATIONS

Library of Congress Cataloging in Publication Data

Lazarus, Sy.
   Loud & clear.

   1. Communication. 2. Nonverbal communication. 3. Communication in
   management. I. Title.
HM258.L36   301.14   75-4925
ISBN 0-8144-05375-9
ISBN 0-8144-7546-9

© 1975 AMACOM

A division of American Management Associations, New York.

First AMACOM paperback edition 1981

For M.A., Susan, and Wendy

PREFACE

In an era of space travel, medical marvels, and technical accomplishment beyond the comprehension of most of us, we experience difficulty making ourselves understood by one another. This inability to communicate affects every conceivable situation in which we're involved.

Exaggerated? Think for a moment about the countless decisions we make and subsequent actions we take that are based on incomplete or erroneous information. The likeliest cause, aside from sheer lack of information, is half-communication. There is an old European adage that says, "Much of our lives is spent in worry, most of it about things that never happen." To paraphrase this, "Much of our days is spent in communication, most of it about things that we never understand."

Beginning with the family environment, communication failures extend into our work, our social activities, various levels of government, and finally relationships between nations. Simple transactions involving two people result in misunderstanding and ill will. Activity is delayed and frustration provoked.

Where barriers of language, custom, or background exist, it is understandable when wires get crossed. But what explanation can we give for confusion when those attempting to communicate share a common language and cultural perspective? What reasons can we furnish our children for our inability to teach them to understand their own words while providing them with the technical expertise to visit other worlds—or destroy their own?

In the late 1960s, shortly after our astronauts had landed on the moon for the first time and stimulated the entire country to contemplate the possibilities of interplanetary travel, I attended a lecture by Max Lerner. I think a comment he made following his talk is pertinent to our subject matter and worth relating.

"Isn't it exciting?" asked one of the students. "Like Columbus discovering the New World!" stated another. Turning to Lerner, a third asked, "Do you think there are intelligent beings on other planets, and can we communicate with them?" "I am not so much concerned about that," replied Lerner, "as I am with a more pressing question: Are there intelligent beings on *this* planet, and can we communicate with *them?*"

This book assumes that the answer to both questions is a cordial yes—followed by some equally emphatic ifs. These are set forth as guidelines in the first five chapters and then applied to specific spheres of daily life, from the closest to the most remote; the final chapter looks at steps that we as a society might take to improve communication in the future.

This book also addresses itself only to communication that fails through inadvertence. Obviously the mastery of even the fine points of transmission and reception is meaningless in the face of outright lying, misrepresentation, or evasion (though Chapter 8 will present some illustrations that skirt close to this last). The fundamentals and applications given in the chapters presume that the communicators are both truthful and as accurate as they know how to be in their transmissions. When one of them is not, all bets are off.

The discussion on these pages is not intended to provide a scholarly examination of communication. It attempts rather to analyze some of the commoner breakdowns that affect our everyday interchanges. Its modest objective is improvement of ability in this universal activity. The approach is meant to be entertaining. If the outcome seems successful to even a small percentage of readers, I will feel that my effort has been justified.

Although a blanket word of appreciation may be rather impersonal, I must use this means to recognize the contributions of the many individuals, some nameless to me and others known, whose slice-of-life episodes provided the basis for this book. My thanks are also due to Mal Sherman, of Zayre Corp., who suggested the approach used in treating this material.

And finally, words of gratitude to the women in my life. Special thanks to my wife, M.A., whose encouragement and assistance helped make this book possible; to my daughters, Susan and Wendy, who were sometimes impossible; to my mother, Elsie, who helped make me possible; and to my sister, I.B., who always was as interested as possible.

Sy Lazarus

CONTENTS

LOUD
and CLEAR

1

BEGINNING WITH BASICS

What is communicating? The barber who names his shop *The Clip Joint* is doing it. A commuter railroad that distributes an understandable revision of its weekly timetable has done it. A look of approval from a parent following a child's accomplishment does it. These things and countless others result in that universally sought but frequently missed objective—communication.

Effectiveness in this art shouldn't be an occasional thing. The isolated incident in which one must muster all resources to get across usually generates more perspiration than illumination. Making the basics of good communication part of everyday routine will provide the reward of new or enhanced rapport. And regular application of the guidelines about to be discussed will instill not only the fundamentals but many of the subtler factors that lead to mastery of the art.

In much of life's activity, anticipation is greater than

realization. With regard to communication, however, it is aftereffect that is most significant. Certainly there are occasions when a person may derive considerable pleasure from the exchange itself, as when speaking marriage vows or learning of a promotion, but the payoff really occurs after comprehension. However great the time and effort expended in disseminating a message, only when it generates the desired outcome has our activity been justified. A simple axiom, to be sure; yet our failure to practice it results in lost hours daily accompanied by confusion, irritation, and sometimes quite unexpected results.

An example that quickly comes to my mind involves a childhood experience (and one of my first encounters with communication problems). My grandmother, visiting us from another state, was to take my sister and me on a downtown shopping trip while my mother kept an appointment at the beauty parlor. Afterward we were all to go to dinner in a local restaurant. My mother announced that we were to meet her at 5 P.M. in front of The Boston Store, a local department store that our family frequently used as a rendezvous point.

While walking through town, we passed The Boston Luncheonette, which my grandmother decided was to be the meeting place. Despite our pleas, Grandma stood her ground. After an hour of fruitless waiting, I volunteered to go to the department store, about two blocks away, to search for my mother. Grandma, who was beginning to waver, agreed, so off I went. Sure enough, Mom was there, and she returned to the luncheonette with me—only to find her mother and her daughter gone. It seems Grandma had realized that the other location was the right one after all and had headed there. When we finally got together at home for a potluck dinner, we analyzed the misunderstandings. In the bright light of comprehension, it was difficult to see why things hadn't been clear in the first place. That foulup was but an early demonstration of how easily even a simple message can misfire.

The nineteenth-century French statesman and writer Alexis de Tocqueville once commented that Americans can talk about everything but cannot converse about anything. This observation succinctly pinpoints a major obstacle to communication: failure to realize that it entails an *interchange*, a two-way contact that *exchanges* information, ideas, or perspectives. What de Tocqueville referred to includes all the graces of a good conversationalist, not the least of which is the ability to listen well. However, listening is only one of numerous considerations that must be kept in mind if we are to establish a circuit. Other factors also have important roles to play, and the most significant ones will be examined in some detail.

Effective communication may be compared with successful participation in athletics. Both depend on proficiency in the fundamentals. Therefore, a review of the basics of both transmitting and receiving is in order before we examine specific aspects of our rather broad subject.

The communication process may be illustrated in simplified form this way:

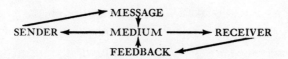

The sender, in transmitting a message to the receiver, employs a medium of conveyance. This vehicle may be selected carefully or used unwittingly. In either case, the receiver's response constitutes feedback to the sender, a kind of return to the source of some of the output. So we have interaction of sender and receiver, or, as true communication has sometimes been defined, an exchange of understanding.

Since we observe at the outset that functioning as a communicator occurs both when sending and when receiving, it becomes desirable to outline first the fundamental components of each of these roles.

Sending the message

Regardless of whether communicating is considered primarily in terms of sending or receiving, almost everyone exerts greater effort when attempting to get a message across than when taking in a transmission. This is due largely to the fact that transmission is active and reception passive, and it is natural to be more involved where action is required.

If the sender is to be successful in conveying his message, he must
   —Know the receiver and present the information at his level.
   —Speak or write clearly and concisely.
   —Convey the desire to reach the receiver by his attitude.
   —Obtain feedback to confirm that the message has been received correctly.

These four simple rules not only dramatically improve one's sending overnight but assure the continuing effectiveness of personal communication.

Rule 1, knowing the receiver, means taking into account

the native language, educational accomplishments, social status, economic level, predispositions (or prejudices), aspirations, and family structure of that receiver. It also means considering barriers to the correct receipt of the message set up by the situation or by interpretation. It enables the sender to choose the word with the proper nuance among several with the same basic denotation as well as to time the transmission effectively. Several of these factors will receive special treatment in the chapters to follow. For the moment let's take a quick look at a few examples.

Suppose you are a man and you are speaking with the leader of a local women's liberation chapter. It might not be very fruitful to invite her opinion on a bathing beauty contest; her office would probably impel her to present the movement's viewpoint on the subject. But if you asked her to discuss women's roles in a changing society, you would very likely elicit a varied and informative answer. This answer will be influenced of course by her own experience. If she is married and has raised children, the thinking will not be that of an unmarried woman who seeks to enter an untraditional marriage. And it will differ still more from that of the woman who has elected to pursue a career and remain single.

A case of the sender's not being attuned to the receiver occurred in an incident involving the late movie mogul Sam Goldwyn. It seems one of his directors told Goldwyn that he was opposed to making a film from a script under consideration because it was "too caustic." "I don't care how much it costs," replied Goldwyn. "If it'll make a good picture, we'll shoot it."

An exchange in which the sender temporarily forgot

the receiver's identity took place during my Air Force days. Our boss, a captain, got upset by a decision his superior made and pleadingly commented, "Colonel, you just can't do that!" To which the good colonel replied, "Captain, I can do anything I damn well please!"

Rule 2 involves the use of basic skills in speaking and writing. The KISS principle—keep it short and simple—is pertinent here. Brevity and simplicity may not win forensic honors, but they warrant paramount consideration in effective communication. The less said (or written), the easier and faster the message is received and the less room exists for misunderstanding. Once when a major-league baseball team was in a slump after losing seven straight games, the local announcer used this phrasing to transmit the news that the contest scheduled for that night had been canceled: "There's no chance of our team losing again tonight," he said. "The game's been rained out." A beautiful case of putting it all together.

The careful sender makes certain a word with multiple meanings—and many have them—gets across with the one intended. Context may insure this. For example, the word *dog* has a variety of meanings, depending on how, when, and where it's used. At the stadium, we ask for a "dog" to order a frankfurter. If we are in a salesman's presence and he refers to a "dog," it's an item that isn't selling well. If you hear that salesman say "My dogs are killing me," you know he's had a hard day covering his territory on foot. Finally, there is the creature who started it all, the household pet.

But context may not help, especially when there is no chance for clarification. What would you do if a traffic policeman shouted to you as your car paused at an intersection, "Go right onto the next street"? And consider this description of a violin concert given by schoolgirls: "The children charmed the eye as well as the ear. Their blue-painted violins and their yellow bows stood out against a cardinal-red backdrop." Where were the bows: on the instruments or in the performers' hair?

Regarding *rule 3*, the noted business consultant and authority on motivation Saul Gellerman says, "Communication depends on the attitude of the sender toward the receiver." * I submit that aside from how the sender regards his receiver, his general attitude is also significant. It is always important to reflect the *right* attitude when attempting communication. *Right* will vary with the receiver involved, the intensity or urgency of the situation, and the emotional atmosphere in which transmission is carried on. But in all cases, sincerity and respect are fundamental. If the sender shows a real desire to reach the receiver and achieve what we may call a mutuality of comprehension, then many barriers to understanding are swept aside, and the recipient of the communication is better tuned in. The receiver seems to detect a feeling-to-content ratio and almost unconsciously extends his antennae. Manifesting good attitude paves the sender's way and helps assure him success by stimulating an alert, positive welcome for his message in the receiver.

An instance comes to my mind that rather forcefully demonstrated the contrary of right attitude. It occurred during a class for international instructors who were being trained to present a program to groups in their own countries. The participant from one of these nations was, like the country he came from, autocratic, and the trainer who

* Saul Gellerman, *Management by Motivation* (AMA, 1968), p. 46.

conducted our presentation tried to make him aware of how an authoritarian style might adversely affect the willingness of his future students to learn.

"You have to make them want to learn this material," said our group leader. "They have to be motivated; you can't just tell them to do it."

"In my country," came the crisp reply, "we can tell them, and they will do as they are told!"

Rule 4 tests whether a receiver has gotten the same message that the sender thinks he has transmitted. Obtaining feedback, or a return of part of the output to the source of the input, is essential if we are to be certain that we have gotten through. This does not guarantee that the receiver will take the action or adopt the thinking requested in the message, which is of course a matter of followup. Feedback will tell us only whether we have communicated—whether our transmission has been received as intended. The accuracy of any communication increases with the amount of feedback, including nonverbal (to be discussed in Chapter 3).

Whenever I'm involved with feedback, I think of an incident that dramatized the effect of its absence. One summer during my school years I worked at an inner-city day camp. I usually assisted in an arts and craft session, where I realized that the instructor was neglecting one of the more talented children in favor of less gifted artists. Most of the children were constantly running up to the instructor to show their handiwork, and he'd comment, "That's pretty good; now see what you can do with this part. . . ."

"Why are you ignoring that little fellow who paints so well?" I asked.

"Oh, he's very good, and I told him so in a long talk we had at the beginning of the summer. Now I'm concentrating on those kids who don't know which end of the paint brush to use," was the reply.

As time passed, I noticed less and less participation by the gifted child. One day I realized that he had stopped painting altogether and was merely gazing out the window. Everyone around him was hard at work.

"Why aren't you painting?" I inquired.

"What for?" he replied.

"Well, you do such nice work," I answered, "and everyone enjoys your pictures." To which he responded, "How do I know that when nobody looks at them?"

There are several approaches we can use to obtain feedback and gain the desired aftereffect. The commonest and certainly most obvious method is to question the receiver on specific points to ascertain his understanding and fathom his empathy. Then there is the general, or open-ended, query. "What do you think?" or "How do you feel about it?" affords the receiver an opportunity to take the sender's role in the communication as well as to show the original sender that they're on the same wavelength. (We'll examine the art of questioning more closely in Chapter 2.) Careful observation of the receiver's facial expressions and manner will also reveal how well the message is being comprehended and then accepted.

In addition, if the consequence of the message involves the receiver in some action, soliciting suggestions from him regarding his participation will certainly aid the interchange. For example, if a parent sends a child to the store for some groceries, asking him what he might like to include in the shopping list does much to enlist his cooperation and increases his interest. (It will no doubt add to the cost of the trip as well.) In short, participative involvement elicits a positive response. Behavioral scientists in fact increasingly confirm its importance in improving morale and productivtiy on the job.

Reversing the role

The task of the receiver is more difficult than that of the sender, for it requires greater patience and effort. It is also a highly cerebral one, because most of the activity takes place above the ears. Some of us—students, children, subordinates, understanding friends—assume the position of receiver on a fairly regular basis. And just as certain considerations make us more effective senders, there are specific skills that help us become better receivers.

Basically, to communicate effectively, the receiver must
—Know the sender and expect the information to come from his level.
—Listen with concentration; avoid distractions.
—Keep an open mind.
—Obtain clarification.

To expand on these points, *rule 1* means that the receiver must attempt to view the message in the light of the sender's identity, experience, and orientations. In sum, the communicators share the responsibility of establishing a common frame of reference. In this connection, an unpleasant episode in the life of my wife's and mine several years ago is illustrative.

It seems that while changing the baby's diaper, she stuck her finger with one of the safety pins and the finger soon got painfully infected. Finally, one afternoon she visited a doctor, who performed some minor surgery in his office to cleanse the wound. "If you suffer any discomfort after the local anesthetic wears off," said the physician, "just take two aspirin." "Aspirin?" she repeated, but she didn't pursue the matter. Well, what she was experiencing by 2 A.M. could be classified as "discomfort" only by an accomplished masochist. She called it the severest pain she had ever had. After a painful and sleepless night, she asked me to contact the physician, who was finally located making morning rounds at a nearby hospital, and a prescription for relief was obtained.

The gap that existed between my wife's perspective and her doctor's professional knowledge should have been recognized by both. But while he can't be let off the hook, his patient also had the obligation to remember that physicians necessarily view a person as "average"—and prescribe medication according to this norm—unless informed otherwise. Apparently forgetting this, she neither asked for further instructions on what to do in case aspirin did not work nor got in touch with him as her pain began to mount.

Failure to concentrate (rule 2) will obviously waste time by requiring the sender to repeat and the receiver to listen again. It is also apparent that the more complex the communication, the greater must be the intensity of concentration. A student attending a class in philosophy or advanced mathematics, for example, needs to listen with more concentration than when attending a campus political rally.

When the business and finance section of *The New York Times* featured an article about the appointment of a new chief executive officer for a department store chain, the heading read, "Lawyer, A Superb Listener, New Chief at Macy's." * The impact of Donald B. Smiley's ability to give undivided attention to anyone speaking with him was the focus of this story. It stated: "Mr. Smiley is a listener, not a big talker. He quietly sizes up people and situations and then acts. Associates who have worked long with him say that he is a superb listener."

Listening has often been equated with intelligence. Some people facetiously observe that one can't display ignorance when silent. And then there's the old professor who commented, "You don't learn anything when you're talking." The passivity of the receiver implied by that crack does not make listening easy, and with good reason. First of all, we listen roughly three times as fast as we speak (650 and 150–175 words per minute respectively). Second, most of us are eager to answer or comment on the message and are often preparing our response even before the sender finishes transmitting. This accounts for our knowing what someone is going to say before the sentence is finished. The practice of one-upmanship, which many people confuse with conversational ability, also has an impact on effective listening. Meaningful listening has been the focus of many business programs and college courses. It could easily be the subject of an entire chapter in this book, and frequent reference will be made to it.

What *rule 3* says is: Put away your predispositions and reaction patterns and take a fresh point of view in each situation. A tough requirement? They don't come any more demanding. It means holding egotism in check, because pride as well as tradition leads most of us to attribute a misunderstanding to sender error; it may just as readily be a case of receiver failure. Also those on the receiving

* Isadore Barmash, *The New York Times* (January 31, 1971).

side of a communication frequently tend to adopt a kind of "All right, show me" or "Let's see you make me understand" attitude, generating even greater pressure on the sender. Make up your mind to be "confused by the facts" and you'll be receptive to what you hear, even when it conflicts with your established ideas.

When a professional hockey coach spoke disparagingly of his players after they had lost a championship game, a reporter asked him if such talk wasn't bad for the team's morale. "I don't think so," replied the coach. "What I'm really trying to do is reach them. Sometimes you live and work so closely with people that you fail to communicate because you are assuming that they know how you feel. If this approach works, then it's been worthwhile." Hopefully the coach knew his men, because his new tack could be successful only if they were open-minded.

Another example involves the effect of conditioning on open-minded reception, and it occurred in my family. One of our pre-teen daughters asked us what happened in the dust bowl during the 1930s. She showed her disbelief as my wife began explaining about soil erosion and the plight of Oklahoma farmers during the Depression years. "Cut it out," she said, in the tone of someone experiencing a put-on. Finally we were able to convince her that the information was really accurate. Her skepticism was understandable; since she was growing up in a home of football fans, her past references to any bowl always involved a stadium. She would have been immediately satisfied had we told her that in 1935, Oklahoma beat Kansas in the Dust Bowl 17 to 6.

Rule 4 of course is the receiver's equivalent of the sender's obtaining feedback. Even though the receiver has listened carefully and believes he has understood the transmission correctly, he may want to verify parts of the message. This is a particularly good idea when it contains considerable detail or concerns an unfamiliar subject. The clarification rule also calls for the receiver to ask for elaboration. If our friend with the infected finger had heeded this as well as rule 1, she would have been spared much suffering.

Despite efforts by all hands to comply with recommended practices, the good ship communication often gets torpedoed because the receiver misinterprets the sender's words. William Bernbach, founder and leading light of the advertising firm of Doyle Dane Bernbach, tells an amusing story that illustrates this point. One particularly cold and stormy winter evening, he arrived at a Midwestern hotel and gratefully took shelter from the elements. After checking into his room, he went to the dining room for dinner. With the chill of the weather still in his bones, he asked the waitress what the *soupe du jour* was, to which she replied she didn't know but would find out. A few minutes later she returned to announce that the *soupe du jour* was the soup of the day. . . . As any student of humor is aware, possible differences of interpretation or double meanings are the swing pin of stories that cause laughter.

Choosing the medium

Finally, there is the medium through which the sender will attempt to reach the receiver. Reach of course implies all the elements that go into getting across, not merely the procedure for contact. Many senders give little if any thought to the means of conveying a message. Yet in many situations, the medium can materially aid or detract from its very receipt—and obviously a message has to arrive before it can be taken in. Almost as obviously, much of the impact of communication is governed by how it travels.

If it is desirable first to alert the receiver to a forthcoming message, perhaps a letter should be used to announce the impending communication. In this way, the sender has set the stage for concentration when the actual exchange gets under way. It doesn't matter whether the communication is done by phone, in person, or through another letter; the receiver is prepared for it. Then too, it is necessary to consider the limitations of a medium. A good speaker who attempts to address a large group in a room without satisfactory sound amplification has doomed the message regardless of the receiver's interest. A radio announcer must become thoroughly familiar with his medium, developing both a technique and a style that will compensate for his invisibility to his audience.

The effective sender selects the medium on the basis not only of how it will be received but also of what works best for him. A shy communicator will not choose face-to-face interaction with a large group. Conversely, the salesman whose writing lacks flair should seek in-person contact with the customers.

The medium need not be verbal. Suppose that a husband and wife have been having a marital quarrel, and both now regret it. Words come hard for both; written sentiment seems awkward and inappropriate. Another form of communication must be attempted. The wife may take the initiative by preparing her husband's favorite meal, while her spouse may demonstrate his feelings with a bouquet of flowers, a gift, or perhaps an old-fashioned kiss on the cheek. Each is an effective message, making an apology

without either a written or a spoken word. Timing is a
particularly important consideration in this type of interchange, as it is in most forms of communication, and more
will be said about this later.

Although spoken communication is the easiest form, it
certainly is not always the best choice. The relationship
between the sender and receiver, their perspectives on the

subject of the communication, each one's life style, and dozens of other factors should be cranked into the decision on which medium will do the job best (and fastest, if that is also desirable). Even when we select verbal communication, we have the choice of using a telephone or meeting in person. If nonverbal supplements are important, we will opt for the latter. We can't read the enthusiasm, excitement, and joy on a person's face when we are not in his or her presence.

When communication involves details and precise information, written words or documented backup to the verbal transmission should be the format. Although the instant feedback that is available from a face-to-face encounter is not present in the written exchange, the opportunity to review and reassimilate that is provided by the written word may offset this lack of immediacy.

The power of the medium impresses me anew each time I present a captionless cartoon in group sessions on improving communication. I ask everyone to write words for the cartoon, and regardless of the number of participants, I rarely wind up with duplication. Even when two people think of the same theme for a caption, their wording is different. This experiment vividly demonstrates how individual interpretation is. It also proves the hazards in taking something visual for granted. Try it out yourself. Use the cartoon on the opposite page with friends or family. In addition to proving the point, it's guaranteed to stimulate the creative impulse and evoke some good laughs. Although a picture may be worth the proverbial thousand words, those words don't mean the same thing to everyone who hears them. Get the picture?

2

FOLLOWING THROUGH

Any communication involves factors that are special to that particular one. Mastery of the fundamentals discussed in Chapter 1, important as they are, does little to accommodate changing considerations from one occurrence to another. Therefore, in addition to a firm grip on the basics of effective sending and receiving, some thought must always be given to the variables operative in any interchange.

An obvious example is timing. A sender adversely affects reception by approaching a receiver who is involved in something important to himself. Speaking to a golfer who is about to sink a putt and interrupting a do-it-your-selfer in the middle of an intricate phase of his project are illustrations of poor timing. In these instances, the receiver isn't so favorably disposed to the incoming transmission as at a moment of free attention.

There are myriad other factors that must be taken into

account in a given communication, ranging from the super-ficial to the profound and from the ordinary to the highly exceptional. One of the most important of these is the intention of each communicator, or what may be called the core of the message.

The tip of the iceberg

The core of a message is what the sender is really trying to say, and it may or may not correspond with the actual content of what he is transmitting to the receiver. Much of our everyday conversation concerns trivia. Nobody who has looked out a window needs the information that it's a bright, sunny day. The surface of such an inter-change—the comment on the weather—has nothing to do with the core, which in most cases is simply an expression of the desire to be sociable.

When initiating a contact, a sender has a predetermined objective in mind, whether conscious or unconscious. If it is conscious, he not only knows the results he is seeking but has mentally structured the response he wants from the receiver. For example, in discussing a family problem with a relative, the sender's objective might be to obtain agree-ment or sympathy, hint at the need for financial aid, or merely get something off his chest.

If the sender is unaware of his true intentions or ex-presses them too subtly, he gives the receiver little chance to identify them correctly. But here too, the receiver has some responsibility. If he is less than perceptive, nothing short of full disclosure (which is ordinarily desirable any-way) will get through to him. In short, a lack of empathy results in communication failure. It could be quite a while before either party recognizes that the exchange has been meaningless.

Effective communication in such cases especially calls for respect and the goodwill that generates respect. This grounding permits directness in both the message and the feedback, which in turn makes true intent clear. Given these conditions, the unmentionable can be discussed and the unthinkable considered.

Senders must be alert to the emotional state of a receiver at the time of transmission. If the receiver is experiencing strong feeling from other causes during the communication, or if a recent encounter has left an emotional residue, it will create a frame of mind unrelated to the present transmission. This altered perspective will not only influence his comprehension but govern his response to the message as well. A person's ego state is one of the primary factors in determining the kind and quality of communication that takes place. Psychiatrists Eric Berne and Thomas A. Harris have demonstrated this tellingly in their best-sellers on transactional analysis.

Receivers need to be equally mindful of psychological forces in themselves. Attitudes, desires, and daydreams prepare us to react in certain ways to communications. Sometimes the swiftness of our response may startle us. Both fools and angels rush in when action is involuntary. We have played out the scene so often mentally that we're not quite sure if this time it's for real. This instant reaction is frequently inappropriate and is certainly not based on adequate evaluation of the incoming message. So the injunction "Count to ten" before sending out feedback applies here.

There are times of course when the core of a message seems objectively quite clear but the receiver is unwilling to take it in. This differs from an outright refusal to give the sender's hoped-for response in that the receiver side-steps the point rather than confronts it. For example, my wife had been nipped at the heel by a rather large dog belonging to neighbors. Afterward she was understandably wary of the animal and uncomfortable whenever it entered our yard. Finally, following a few more visits by their pet, I approached the owner and requested plainly and unambiguously that he please keep it off our premises. He said he understood how my wife felt in the dog's presence and tried to assure me that his pet had probably forgotten the incident entirely. I then indicated to him that since I couldn't discuss the matter with his dog, there was really no way we could be certain of this fact. As I was clearly going to get no feedback to the core of my message, our conversation was terminated.

Another distortion of communication consists in obscuring not the core of the message but the sender's identity. People will sometimes plead their case or express their opinion using someone else as the point of reference. For example, a supervisor may direct his boss's attention to a worthy subordinate who deserves a raise, citing merits that oddly enough closely parallel those the supervisor feels he has himself. This constitutes a kind of transmutation of communication, attributing one's own situation to another and thereby making a point without commitment.

It might take an astute receiver to interpret the supervisor's transmission correctly, but many similar disguises are transparent: the teenager who seeks assistance from a venereal disease clinic for "a friend," or the businessman who asks his doctor what he thinks about a certain diet that "someone at work" has tried. In the following conversation, the subterfuge is about as subtle as a child's blaming an empty cookie jar on the cat:

HUSBAND Let me tell you about the gift one of the guys at the office bought his wife for their wedding anniversary.

WIFE Who, honey?

HUSBAND That's not the point. It's what he got her that I'm talking about.

WIFE What was it?

HUSBAND On his last trip to the Coast, he visited an antiques shop, knowing how this junk turns his wife on.

WIFE I wouldn't call all antiques junk.

HUSBAND Well, you tell me what you think of this one. He bought a cupola for the roof of their house.

WIFE I'm not sure you're *all* wrong when you call antiques junk! If he'd brought back a weather vane, it might have been a little more practical.

HUSBAND Oh, you like those roosters with the arrows that turn in the wind?

WIFE Well, all weather vanes aren't like that, but it's something I think I'd like for our house.

If husband and wife have been married for any length of time and if their communication has been moderately effective, each one realizes perfectly well what the other is doing. In such a case, disguised transmittal serves a purpose. However, it's usually desirable to eliminate the third party and deal directly with the receiver.

Saying it right

There is little doubt that ability to articulate will influence the quality of communication. Limited or undeveloped skill in this area can adversely affect sending ability. Articulate delivery merely means "telling it like it is," but that isn't always a simple thing to do.

One problem is that certain expressions have emotionally negative connotations that can undermine our message if we use them heedlessly. Such words as *radical, stupid, lazy,* and *stubborn* can make our point or lose our receiver. If we know our receiver and can judge his views on a given subject, we are on safer ground when using negatively charged expressions.

Conversely there are pleasant words that create desirable images in the receiver's mind. *Dependable, honest, conscientious, helpful,* and *sincere* are a few of an almost endless list of terms that make an agreeable impression. Some words carry various and even opposing connotations, depending on their context. "An old-fashioned apple pie" and "an old-fashioned washing machine" create very different images.

Alternate phrasing can help reorient attitudes, even those that seem part and parcel of a particular function. An example is the title of a booklet for supervisors I saw recently. Instead of "How to Give Orders," it's called "How to Issue Instructions." Before the reader opens the cover, a foundation has been laid for a special perspective on his job. How an idea is worded is as significant as the idea itself.

Even a necessarily negative message such as a criticism or correction can be made more palatable by the simple device of depersonalizing it. By referring to *"the* problem" instead of *"your* problem" or *"a* difficulty" as opposed to "the difficulty *you* have," the sender can reduce the subjectivity of his message and make it more acceptable to the receiver. The more delicate and potentially painful the communication, the greater the need to help the receiver keep an open mind. Material that might generate considerable friction can be transmitted without penalty simply by the way it is relayed. This point is illustrated by the famous line from *The Virginian*, "When you call me that, smile!"

Sometimes the very placement of a word in a sentence can distort the sender's intent and impede his message. This is easier to spot in writing, though it is commoner in oral delivery because of the greater speed of speech. Chapter 4 will give some examples of this booby trap. Other times, choosing one of two words with closely related meanings will send the message awry. That happened to me not long ago at the dentist's:

"There's a sensitivity under that filling when I chew," I related.

After taking X-rays and completing his examination, he commented, "I can't find a thing, but there may be an air space in there conducting the sensation."

"It might just be your observation," I replied.

"There's nothing wrong with my observation!" came the snappy retort.

The dentist thought me critical of his professional ability because he defined *just* as *merely* or *only*. My use of the word meant *indeed*, and my intent was to praise his judgment. I was really saying, "That could be the reason."

The omission of only a few words can cause misinterpretation. There was the time I phoned a relative to state,

"I'll be in Minneapolis next week." The receiver interpreted this to mean the entire week, while my visit was
actually scheduled to last three days. Obviously the addition of "for a few days" or "from Sunday night through
Wednesday afternoon" would have provided the clari-

*Now, Mr. Edwards, I know that you believe you understand
what you think I have said, but I'm not sure
you realize that what you hear is not what I mean.*

fication necessary for instantaneous identical comprehension.

Humorous stories are filled with laughs based on the placement and interpretation of a word. Try this one:

DOCTOR   Is your cold any better?

COUNTRY BILL   Nope!

DOCTOR   Did you follow my instructions and drink some orange juice after the hot bath?

COUNTRY BILL   Nope! After drinking the hot bath, I couldn't get any orange juice down.

This wasn't the first time Country Bill had had problems with a message. He was a portrait painter, and one day he received an offer of $2,500 from a lady in Omaha who wanted him to paint her in the nude. The price was right, so Bill agreed. But he did set one condition—"that I be allowed to wear my socks so I'll have some place to put the brushes."

As a warden said in that movie a few years back, "What we have here is a failure to communicate!"

Of course, comprehension is contingent on the contemporary vernacular. Many fluent, verbally skillful people would be hard-pressed to communicate with some of today's youth. Although ostensibly speaking the same language as they do, an older receiver might require an interpreter if his ears met with the following three-way interchange:

"Hey, man, if that's your bag and it turns you on, then do your own thing."

"I'd get uptight being into that."

"Let me lay it on you! It's out of sight, man—it'd make you flip. Like it offs the hangups, dig?"

"No way! It takes too much bread to split."

"My vibes tell me you're copping out."

"Maybe, but all you guys do is rap, and that's no scene for a bad dude. I want to find out where it's at."

For those of us who "turn on" the radio, eat "bread," and "rap" on the door, it may require some effort to "dig" (the meaning, not a ditch). Perhaps not so much as it might have a few years ago, however, for many of the words in this simulated conversation have become part of our vocabulary, used in print and on television and probably soon to show up in the dictionary. This brings up a key consideration: "Saying it right" varies, with the locale, age, and relationship of the communicators all playing an important part in achieving mutual understanding.

Telling it like it isn't

Young people who create a special vocabulary are in fact reflecting a widespread practice among their elders: trade jargon. Some of it is valid terminology that answers the special technical needs of a given craft, profession, or industry. But much of it consists of expressions that are used unnecessarily in place of commoner, better-understood terms.

A recent experience with this occurred when I visited our family physician's office for an annual examination. The doctor requested me to return for a few tests, so on my way out, I stopped at the nurse's desk and asked for a second appointment. "You'll need two blocks," she said. For a confused moment, I attempted to figure this statement out: What size would these blocks be, and how would they be used? Then I made an absolutely brilliant response. "What did you say?" I inquired. "You'll need two blocks—I mean two time periods," she replied, realizing the confusion generated by her initial remark. It developed that each standard 15-minute appointment was referred to as a block of time on the doctor's schedule.

Since embarking on the era of the acronym, business has had a field day consolidating first initials to form slick terms and catchy new words. Unfortunately, in many cases, the quality of in-company communication is adversely affected. The use of acronyms in World War II triggered the population explosion of them in the world of work. It was a short step from RADAR (radio detecting and ranging) and SNAFU (situation normal—all fouled up) to PERT (program evaluation reporting technique) and PIP (profit improvement program).

The problem with acronyms is the same as with all other trade jargon—it requires learning unnecessary substitutes for more familiar terms. To be sure, this hasn't discouraged any organizations from fabricating and using acronyms, but occasional thought might be given to the effect on the uninitiated receiver's comprehension of the message.

Misunderstandings may arise for the identical reason from the use of first letters to form initials (sort of second-class, because they lack the cleverness and humor of their more popular relatives). One example of an old standard presented some difficulty for me on my first job. The employer had established an Executive Development Program (EDP), run by the training department to which I belonged. Once, when requested to take some forms to EDP for processing, I turned them over to someone in my department's EDP section. After he had had a few good laughs, I was told the forms were meant for the Electronic Data Processing Department.

But let's get back to the more elegant acronym. Today we have divisions at all levels of a company outdoing each other in their efforts to create fresher and catchier acronyms. A current fad in human relations training is TA (transactional analysis). One major airline has a TACT program (transactional analysis in customer treatment), and a retail organization has TAPE (transactional analysis program for executives). It almost seems there's a department tucked under a stairwell someplace whose main function is to make up acronyms. It's headed by an APE (acronym producer extraordinary) who graduated from the company's FREAC (fast-rising executives and comers) program.

Every business has its jargon. In retailing, for instance, the word *turn* refers to annual merchandise turnover, or the number of times a particular item—say, undershirts—is sold during a 12-month period. In showing a newly hired clerk how to maintain a department, an experienced supervisor said, "We turn this merchandise four times a year." The clerk thought the job involved flipping the items to their opposite side every three months to keep dust from settling in.

Radio and television have promos (promotional spot announcements). The transportation industry has FOB (free on board) and LTL (less than truckload). But perhaps the most familiar examples of trade language come out of the diner. "BLT down," calls the waitress to the sandwich man, followed by "One wimpy, slice of raw; cow juice," and "A special—burn it and scratch the tomato!"

The art of clarification

Many of the snafus in communication just described could have been untangled by a single question, as my experience in the doctor's office showed. Asking good, effectively worded questions can be as useful to a communicator as it is to a courtroom lawyer. Basically, questions fall into two categories: open-ended and structured.

Open-ended questions permit the other person to answer in broad terms and to determine the length of the reply. "Why did you go?" and the ever-popular "What happened?" are examples of open-ended questions. This type of inquiry is general in nature, can be answered as the receiver wishes, and therefore is relatively acceptable to him; it puts little pressure on him. In both social and business settings, it's customary (and desirable) to start an exchange with open-ended questions.

Structured questions make the respondent feel more constrained and can evoke discomfort and even antagonism, particularly if the questioning is one-sided. The questioner begins to sound like the trial lawyer just referred to, and it is only a matter of time before the examinee will become resentful. Examples of structured questions are "What distracts you?" and "Will you describe the two ways this can be accomplished?" Of course, questions can be so highly structured that they permit only one-word answers. For example, "Are you ready to go?" and "Do you like chili?" allow little room for commentary.

When we are receivers attempting to obtain clarification, our questions will usually be highly structured. But if we are initiating social communication, it is likely that we will pose open-ended questions. "How did you like your trip to San Francisco?" is the sort of icebreaker that provides recognition as well as the opportunity for unlimited response.

Some people are extremely adept at asking them because they do it routinely in the course of their work. Physicians, policemen, scientists, and the already mentioned lawyers are a few examples. Let us now add another group to this list—good communicators.

In the following dialog, several kinds of questions in a variety of shadings comprise the conversation.

DENTIST What seems to be your problem? (*Open-ended*)
PATIENT One of my upper teeth is sensitive.
DENTIST Which tooth? (*Structured*)
PATIENT Second from the back on this side.
DENTIST When does it bother you? (*Moderately structured*)
PATIENT Sometimes while I'm eating sweets.
DENTIST Just sometimes? (*More structured*)
PATIENT I guess it's all the time.
DENTIST Does it bother you any other time? (*Highly structured*)
PATIENT No.
DENTIST Well, let's have a look.

Later:

DENTIST I think we'll clean that out and refill it. (*Income-producing*)
PATIENT Are you going to give me an anesthetic? (*Highly structured*)
DENTIST Well, I won't hurt you. (*Misleading*)
PATIENT I have a low tolerance for pain. (*Chicken*)

DENTIST   If there's one thing you're more concerned with than having your teeth fixed when you come here, it's not suffering. (*Accurate and patient-losing*)

Each sort of question has its advantages and disadvantages, including one type that is really a statement in question form: the rhetorical question. It is commonly used for the irony that can be loaded into it, but this device can backfire. An illustration involves a letter to the editor of a local newspaper. The writer expressed criticism of a reporter who injected commentary into some of the stories by asking, "Is Mr. Smith now writing editorials?" The reply, which appeared under the reader's letter, assured the letter writer that Mr. Smith did not pen the paper's editorials, only those stories under his byline. The correspondent could of course have phrased the question so its meaning was explicit: "Why is Mr. Smith editorializing in his news articles?" for instance. On the other hand, though the editor responding was as entitled as anyone to interpretational error (or deliberate evasion of the core of the message), a more accurate reading might have been made by one whose livelihood depends on astute evaluation of meaning.

A commoner conversational obstacle is created by the questioner who poses a double question whose answers cannot be identical. An example is the wife who asks her husband, "Shall I prepare dinner, or are you eating out tonight?" In most cases, the response to the first part of the question is on the way before the second half is asked, which makes for confusion at least or annoyance at worst. Second example: "Will you be able to finish mowing the lawn this morning, or shall I help you?"

Another kind of double question offers the possibility of a single answer to both parts but can also provoke the receiver if he wants to give a different answer to each. Consider this bit of mild coercion from a husband to his wife: "Will you be near the tobacco store today, and can you buy some pipe cleaners for me?"

The able use of questions to obtain clarification or feedback is of great value because it not only resolves confusion or conflict but also prevents many a problem from occurring.

3

WITHOUT A WORD

Kinesics—which is the study of how we communicate by physical gestures and mannerisms, or "body language" —is a word that has been appearing more and more frequently.

Recent studies at Oxford University's Institute of Experimental Psychology have demonstrated that nonverbal signals constitute a kind of silent language that has a powerful effect on others. Contemporary writing is beginning to explore this phenomenon, called nonverbal communication, and to alert us to its inherent potential and hazards.*

Although most of us are aware of how body movements, gestures, and facial expressions emphasize or qualify our conversation, we give little thought to the implicit

* Julius Fast, *Body Language* (New York: M. Evans and Company, 1970).

communication contained in these actions, independent of the words that may accompany them.

A high school teacher, for example, who may be familiar with all other good communication practices, can dissipate effectiveness through distracting mannerisms, such as tossing a piece of chalk in a game of flip-and-catch. The best of receivers will find their eyes focused on the instructor's hand, their concentration diverted from the message aimed at their ears.

A former associate of mine and fellow instructor exemplified the skillful use—and perception—of nonverbal communication. After he had conducted a session with a difficult group some years back, I asked him how things went. Without uttering a word, he extended his right hand with the palm up and slowly closed it, indicating that the class was in the palm of his hand. A few weeks later, when I knew he had made a presentation to another group known to be particularly disagreeable and hard to motivate, I inquired about the success of his session. This time he not only held out his hand and slowly closed it but then put it in his pants pocket. This additional action signified complete control—that he had the participants not merely in hand but in the bag. His gestures later became an integral part of our regular conversations, adding color, humor, and emphasis to the verbal communications.

Just as this effective instructor knew when he had the class tuned in on his presentation, he was aware also of times when he was beginning to lose them. He read this from telltale gestures and expressions like blank stares resembling an advanced state of somnambulism, limp and slumped posture, sporadic toe tapping and rhythmic pencil pounding. When he perceived such signs of boredom or lack of concentration, my colleague knew that he had to take steps to regain the group's interest, which he would proceed to do by calling a break, changing his pace, asking questions, or whatever he felt was most appropriate to the situation. Signals that he had recaptured the participants' attention included alert eye contact, questions and comments from them, facial expressions that reacted to what was happening, and erect body positions. My associate was universally considered an excellent instructor, in large part, I am certain, because of his nonverbal abilities.

Nonwords shout

Nonverbal communication isn't limited to movements and expressions; it can be read in the places where people choose to be seen, the furnishings they have bought for their homes or offices, and the clothes they wear. Crossed wires frequently result, in fact, from a person's inaccurate reception and processing of incoming nonverbal information, which in turn can prompt him to send inappropriate signals in response. For example, a driver who is flagged down by a police car usually thinks he will have to answer for some traffic violation, though he may not be aware of what his infraction is, and his manner will reflect a reluctant penitence. When he discovers, however, that the officer merely wants to warn him about a loose registration plate, he assumes an entirely different attitude. His assumption that the policeman was acting in his law-enforcement capacity set in motion physical reactions that proved inappropriate to the actual situation.

Nor is nonverbal transmission limited to individuals; business and other organizations also engage in it. Retail merchants continually make wordless statements in their window displays and the type of merchandise stocked inside their stores. They are communicating fashion, change of season, quality, and any of a dozen other messages. A hotel telegraphs its essence by its location, decor, room rates, service, facilities, and reputation. There isn't anything that won't convey a communicative impression, unless it is the philosophical tree that didn't make a sound when it fell because nobody was in the forest to hear it come down.

In stricter definition, however, nonverbal communication consists of the actions of one person directed toward one or more others. And actions shout. Anyone who has traveled on New York City subways is aware of the impact a fellow passenger's actions can have, unmistakably conveying feelings, attitudes, and desires. From the assault of the football lineman whose movements say, "I want on this train," to the underground Don Juan seeking body contact and vicarious romance during the rush hour, every rider's actions communicate feelings and predict behavior.

Investigations of the nature and source of nonverbal transmission trace it to the animal world, and those who have animals in their lives can confirm this through ordinary observation. Everyone is familiar with how a dog displays its teeth in anger, often accompanying this by the vocal signal of growling. A cat's tail and fur rise and it arches its back when frightened; this defensive posture has become a Halloween hallmark. Such commonplace actions on the part of a pet communicate its attitude or problem very clearly.

One of the best-known signals that dogs give to their human family is their scratching on the door when they

want to go outside. When I was a youngster, we had a
white spitz whose expressions of excitement on greeting
one of us included jumping up and down, touching the
person with her front paws, and wetting the floor. As soon
as my father became familiar with this pattern of welcome,
he accommodated the lack of bladder control by arranging
to have the dog meet him outdoors whenever he had been
away for a few days.

Probably the most welcome kinesic communication our
pets send us is the cuddling they do. This silent language

Look! I think she's trying to tell us something.

of affection is probably the major reason for the popularity of our household companions. Through physical proximity and touch, they satisfy a deep human need and provide a constant example by their consistent friendliness, cooperativeness, and dependability.

Perhaps it is this rapport between man and his pets that prompted the late Walt Disney to give personality to his animated cartoon animals, complete with not only the facial expressions and body movements found in humans but also the full range of our emotions, negative as well as positive. These reflections of our own mannerisms from the giant screen surely account for the great popularity that this form of entertainment quickly achieved and continues to have.

In the world of wild animals, there is also an array of movements that communicate feelings, anticipated events, or planned pack activities. Anyone who has watched films taken by hidden cameras recording the daily life of any undomesticated animal is impressed by the physical language the creature generates. There is no intended deception, and misunderstanding is rare. Here of course is where the nonverbal communication of nature's more basic children differs from that of man.

In the human realm, people's everyday existence is replete with examples of nonverbal transmission of thoughts, states of mind, and temporary feelings. Not long ago, my daughter Wendy asked me why I was sticking my tongue out as I did some painting around the house. Without realizing it, I had been engaging in a rather widespread expression of concentration. On analyzing it, I determined in my case, it's limited to concentration during a physical rather than a mental effort. Never have I been observed with tongue protruding while writing, for example, but I've been seen (and have noticed others) with extended tongue while repairing a bicycle or adjusting a household appliance. So Wendy is now aware that when she spots someone in this pose, the person is deeply engrossed in the activity at hand.

When visiting a dentist's office, we convey tension and apprehension by the way we grip the arm rests of the chair. If this tight hold is combined with other indications of concern, such as rigid legs, anxious facial expression, and perhaps perspiration on the forehead, the dentist would be well advised to relax us by using some method besides continuous conversation. Perhaps an exercise in role reversal might make the good tooth doctor realize what he's subjecting us to. We might seat him in a barber's chair, steaming towel on his face, and have the barber barrage him with comments he can't discuss and questions he's unable to answer. The fair play of turnabout dictates that our barber friend then develop a sensitivity in his lower molar.

An attorney should similarly fathom our anxiety about the matter we bring to him so that he may at least dispel the doubt often underlying this feeling. Ordinarily an appraisal of our case and our chances of prevailing in it will do the trick. If he is astute enough to observe our movements and expressions, he should begin to work on putting us at our ease even as he draws out the particulars of our complaint. How many lawyers expend this effort to build confidence and thereby set the stage for smooth communication? As pointed out in *How to Read People Like a*

Book, most attorneys—trial lawyers, anyway—are extremely sensitive to nonverbal messages from a prospective juror.* Clients should be able to expect them to apply this skill with equal intensity in the initial consultation.

Using body language

To focus again on the animal-human relationship for a moment, one of the few circumstances in which we intentionally use nonverbal messages is in communicating with the family pet. Snapping the fingers, clapping the hands, and stamping a foot all have meaning to a dog if these actions have been taught it. Rolling a newspaper or magazine can be threatening to a pet even when not accompanied by angry words. As any animal owner knows, it may be conditioned to respond to a variety of human movements and gestures, and highly trained dogs can send messages by way of a wide range of actions.

Some of us may be familiar with a theme often used in television sketches showing an auto mechanic who stirs up deep concern in a car owner after examining his vehicle. The owner's apprehension intensifies with each question he asks because of the mechanic's nonverbal responses. Here's my version of how the exchange develops:

OWNER   That bad, huh?
MECHANIC   [Shakes his head slowly from side to side.]
OWNER   How long will it take to fix it?
MECHANIC   [Raises his eyebrows.]
OWNER   Any idea of the cost?

* Gerard I. Nierenberg and Henry H. Calero, *How to Read People Like a Book* (New York: Hawthorn Books, Inc., 1971) pp. 156–157.

MECHANIC   [Shrugs his shoulders.]

OWNER   Maybe I should start thinking about buying a
    new car!

MECHANIC   [Extends his arms outwards, palms up.]

OWNER   Call you later to see when it'll be ready.

MECHANIC   [Nods his head and sighs.]

Although only the owner did any talking, the mechanic certainly has communicated, even though his messages leave the owner spinning his wheels in indecision.

While we're on the subject of automobiles, the absence
of nonverbal communication plays a dramatic role in ac-
cidents. Suppose I'm waiting at an intersection to turn in
front of oncoming traffic, and one of the cars approaching
me likewise stops to cross my lane. We must indicate to
each other who will go first. If I wave my hand to him,
I am telling him to precede me. Without such a signal,
however, he must check my facial expressions while watching for any forward motion of my car. Should such an
encounter occur in the dark on a poorly lit road, only the
movement of my vehicle will communicate my intentions.
Automobile operators gamble daily in nonverbal interchanges of this sort.

If all drivers realized that they commit themselves to
automotive Russian roulette whenever they get behind the
wheel, they would make it a point to become more alert
to nonverbal communication and use it more effectively
themselves. A growing awareness in the practice of driving
could generate greater sensitivity in other activities where
speaking is done without words.

Many examples could be cited of similar exchanges
where cues must be derived from wordless communication

—situations involving anything from acute danger to mild frustration. The need to recognize the nonverbal components of such regular actions as crossing the street, riding a bicycle, and waiting in line moves from the category of the peripheral toward the essential as the numbers of participants increase. The complexity of the event is not a major consideration; satisfying and safe involvement are.

In this connection, most of us could profit by observing the sports world, which has long used body language. Baseball fans are aware of the signals a pitcher sends his catcher through a nod of the head or a flick of a finger. A base runner gets the message when the pitcher turns his head toward him before delivering the next pitch. In football, the defense reads a forthcoming play from the offensive alignment. The basketball feint by a ball carrier moving downcourt is designed to mislead the player guarding him and constitutes deception in nonverbal communication, a subject we'll turn to next. Then too, athletes may direct a nonverbal message to critical fans through gestures that have nothing to do with the game, though the coverage provided by television is reducing the frequency of this sort of gesture. Thus we readily understand and accept wordless communication in sports, but it still remains little used in everyday life—except by those who resort to it, legitimately or illegitimately, for purposes of illusion.

Some actions are designed to cover up deceit or insincerity. For example, someone trying to consummate a fraud might conceal his intentions by acting poised, interested, and helpful. Here of course we are entering the domain of the con man, an expert in deceptive practices. When a confidence artist goes into action, giveaway signs of nervousness or deception are conspicuously absent: No lines of tension crease the brow; eyes are purposely set in a calm glaze; there is no awkward or wary set to the shoulders to signal that something may be amiss. Extreme pleasantness, deferential gestures, and a flashing smile are also associated with the super salesman, whose persuasiveness has helped make the expression *caveat emptor* a household word.

The stage and screen are legitimate arenas for kinesics; one form of theater, mime, has taken body language to the level of high art. But actors and actresses can dramatically illustrate the difference between the performance personality and the real self. Many a newspaper story has described incidents involving stars who exhibit markedly different behavior off the stage from what is usually associated with them because of the types of roles they are identified with. Although it may come as a shocking disappointment to their fans, it demonstrates how actions create and maintain an image.

Skillful nonverbal communication need not be the preserve of professional illusionists. Everyone is capable of developing the command of this innate gift as have the people whose use (and abuse) of it I have described. The study of messages without words, though a relatively new field, is expanding rapidly. While the science of kinesics will continue to explore and analyze it, we can gain much from information already available to us—and from simple observation. Watch family members, including your pet if you have one. Watch passersby in the street. And watch yourself. You'll enjoy it.

4

PARDON, MY WRITING IS SHOWING

When I entered the local branch of a chain ice-cream parlor recently, I noticed a sign that read:

WE ONLY SERVE OUR OWN COLA

The order of the words, with the modifier *only* before the word *serve*, conveyed the impression that this establishment offered nothing but cola to its patrons—a practice designed to invite rapid business failure (even with the high profit on liquid refreshment). What the sign intended to say of course was that the chain served its brand exclusively, which means the wording should have been

WE SERVE ONLY OUR OWN COLA

Poor word order within a sentence contributes almost as much to bad written communication as do misplaced phrases. In this connection, a field manager once sent this notice to the supervisor of a subordinate installation: "In order to complete a report for the government, I must know how many employees you have at your plant broken down by sex." To which the supervisor responded, "Our problem here is alcohol!" In this case, a dangling phrase joined our old bugaboo interpretation to short-circuit the transmission.

Construction—and destruction

If we think of a writer as a builder and his communication as an edifice of understanding, we can visualize clear writing as a step-by-step construction process.

Initially the writer functions as an architect, planning the purpose of his communication. Stating that he must determine his purpose before preparing his material is basic enough to trigger the uninspired comment, "So what else is new?" Yet people frequently place their thoughts on paper before determining the objective of their effort. Defining the desired goal provides a blueprint for both construction and writing style. Just as importantly, it crystallizes the communicator's thinking on his subject.

Next, the writer becomes a draftsman, putting the elements of his structure down on paper in accordance with his blueprint. This step organizes all the ideas and puts them in sequential order. When the writing is long or contains much detail, a second, third, or even further draft may be desirable.

The writer now becomes a laborer doing the actual work involved in building that edifice of understanding. In this phase, paragraphs may be considered the beams and words the bricks that complete the structure. Punctuation (which we shall discuss later in this chapter) provides the couplings and supports that solidify and differentiate the structural members. If the writer has worked with application from his plan down to his last nail, there can be no misunderstanding what he has built or the purpose it is intended to serve.

To reverse the analogy, a writer who doesn't approach communication in this manner will very likely end up building a Tower of Babel, even granting that the structure is ever completed. His intentions will be undecipherable and his creation marginally useful. Indeed the builder himself may have difficulty determining what it is he has tried to construct.

One pitfall that many beginning writers fall into is the notion that they must sound impressive. This leads to verbosity. Rather than seeking the shortest, most direct, and most easily understood phrasing, the neophyte attempts long, circuitous rhetoric filled with snobbish synonyms. Moreover, while he readily incorporates popular or informal wording into his conversation, he would not dream of including these same usages in his writing. For some reason, the written word must be pompous.

Lurking behind every sentence of a written communication are other hidden saboteurs that can dilute impact, alter intent, or destroy credibility. Sometimes a desire to appear forceful comes across as antagonistic, or an attempt to be humorous misfires—raising questions in the reader's mind about the writer's psychological stability. If we proofread our message trying to evaluate it through the reader's eyes, we can spot and banish some of these saboteurs.

In addition to polishing specific messages, this exercise

will improve our writing. As in everything else we do, practice in composition makes perfect. But it must be the *right kind* of practice oriented toward the goal of the activity; repetition of and by itself merely reinforces the particular way something is done. In written communication, that goal is to win the receiver's acceptance of the words we commit to paper. If a receiver senses the writer's sincerity and his desire to get the message across, then grammatical slips, poor word choice, and misleading punctuation may have no detrimental effect or may even go unnoticed. On the contrary, if the writer displays an attitude that the reader resents, then appropriate words, clarity, and strength of construction all will fail to get the message across.

If few people would dispute the claim that good writing skills enhance the penetration of a message, fewer still would argue against the statement that bad writing, or lack of writing skill, can be infuriating because it results in misinformation, misinterpretation, and even utter confusion. Two prime examples of confusing transmission are the insurance policy and do-it-yourself assembly instructions. These sources remind me of a drunk leaning against a lamppost—getting more support for himself than illumination for his pathway.

Regarding the first, take this actual example from an auto insurance policy:

> The limit of the company's liability for loss shall not exceed the actual cash value of the property, or if the loss is on a part thereof the actual cash value of such part, at time of loss, nor what it could then cost to repair or replace such property with other of like kind and quality, less depreciation and deductible amount applicable.

What all that means simply is that if your car is involved in an accident, the insurance company will pay you the current resale value of the car after subtracting the deductible amount, reimburse repair costs, or replace your vehicle with an acceptably similar one. Is it any wonder that a majority of policyholders fail to comply with the request printed on the front of their forms, "Please read your policy"? But good news from the offices of state insurance commissioners: They are presently taking a hard look at the language used in all types of policies sold within their states.

Whenever I attempt to put a toy or household article together following the "easy-to-understand" instructions that accompany the dozens of pieces in the package, I am reminded of an incident that occurred during my college days. A friend had invited me to visit his home for the weekend. The residence was presided over by an older woman who was a combination cook, housekeeper, and sitter for the family's eight-year-old daughter. My friend asked me to help him assemble a gym set he had bought for this younger sister's birthday. After carefully laying out all the parts, we started to put the structure together. Several hours later, we ran into a snag and decided to visit the hardware store where the set had been purchased and ask for clarification and advice.

When we returned, the gym had been assembled—by the housekeeper. Knowing that she was barely literate, my friend was hard-pressed to understand how she had handily accomplished what had confused two college students. "How did you do it, Lottie?" he inquired. "Well," she said, "when you can't read too good, you just have to be able to think more."

Grammar & company revisited

One of the commonest termites in the edifice of under-standing is the recurring pronoun with more than one possible antecedent. To illustrate:

They had all the earmarks of a maze, but he said he would explain where they went.

Now consider this revision:

The instructions had all the earmarks of a maze, but John said the hardware clerk would explain where these screws went.

The second sentence shows us that the pronouns *they* and *he* in the first sentence referred to different nouns each time they were used. Of course this ambiguity is also prevalent in spoken communication, but the opportunity to obtain clarification by questioning is unavailable in writing. (Still, I *have* occasionally seen a frustrated reader talking to his reading matter!)

Even if both pronouns in the illustration had referred to the same thing, it would still have behooved the writer to specify their meaning rather than leave it to the reader's interpretation. Pronouns have their place, but the careful writer should avoid using any one with more than one possible antecedent in a sentence.

Many writers avoid first-person pronouns in an attempt to imply humility and thereby gain the reader's goodwill. The use of *I*, however, can pinpoint meaning, lend balance, and provide an occasional reminder of the writer's identity. A piece of writing that is structured entirely in the third person can seem aloof, lacking in intimacy and intensity.

Well-selected verbs make a sentence clear and strengthen the overall message. Unlike many adjectives,

verbs leave little doubt of their meaning. Adverbs used to
modify them affect their power, of course. For example,
"Remove the animal immediately," is not quite the same as
"Remove the animal quickly." The sender of a written
communication can therefore unnecessarily cloud the message by choosing an adverb that might weaken its impact.
Also the use of the active rather than the passive voice will
aid understanding as well as provide supplemental information. Compare "Joe painted the porch last Saturday" with
"The porch was painted last Saturday."

Although the short, direct statement was recommended
in Chapter 1 as the safest vehicle for getting a message

across, there are times when complex sentences are desirable. In these, correct punctuation makes the word units fit smoothly, while its misuse creates obstacles and even detours to understanding.

For many people, punctuating means simply sprinkling on commas; where they should go is a secondary matter. Like an uncertain artist adding a dash of shading to a finished painting, the comma amateur drops one in here and there as a finishing touch. However, the arbitrary placement of this most common of the in-sentence symbols usually creates a stumbling block rather than support railing.

A few simplified rules governing the comma indicate that it should be used to

1. Separate independent clauses or elements of a sentence, each containing a subject and a verb:
   —*My doctor has kept me in bed for a week, but he's not doing me any good.*

2. Separate three or more elements (single words or groups of words) within a series:
   —*He's prescribed pills, vitamins, liquids, and rest.*
   —*I've taken my medicine and vitamins, drunk lots of juice, and gotten plenty of sleep.*

3. Set off dependent clauses or phrases of many sorts from the main sentence:
   —*Unfortunately, in my case, the pills also have a few side effects.*
   —*Since I don't appear to be recovering or even feeling better, I guess I'll have to change doctors.*

These are only three of several dozen overall rules for using the comma that authorities have put forth. Note that most of the commas in the examples create pauses in the same places where they would occur in the spoken sentences. Generally, if you are uncertain whether a comma is needed, don't throw one in.

No mystery surrounds terminal punctuation, but writers are often reluctant to use question marks and exclamation points. Sentences with end punctuation other than a period provide variety and emphasis and thus strengthen written communication, but the alternate marks obviously also influence interpretation. For example, the meaning of the following declarative sentence changes dramatically with the end punctuation: "I'm a nature lover." Or: "I'm a nature lover?"

"That's not what I had in mind..."

Although written communication offers less chance for feedback than oral exchange, it can get return messages. A friend lost, poor cooperation from a club or church group, a small order from a good customer all tell us something about the effect of our writing. Sensitivity to people is important; so is sensitivity to the specific circumstances surrounding them when they receive a communication. A reader's usual reaction pattern can be altered by a change in his thinking that invalidates the writer's concept of him. This means that the writer must always evaluate not only the reader as a person but also the specific conditions affecting him at the time the message comes to him.

It's also helpful to remember that the receiver's image of the sender has considerable bearing on how a written message is accepted and interpreted as well as on the ultimate consequences it produces. Obviously the initial reaction to any writing is based on the identity of the sender.

Even before the communication itself gets read, the reader's ideas about its originator have set the stage for its treatment. And although it is difficult for a writer to always know the place he holds in his receiver's esteem, he ordinarily has some general notion of it. This knowledge must be applied to the nature and wording of the message if the writing is to get a fair hearing.

In the case of a written response to our written communication, the feedback is more apparent. However, the original sender becomes a receiver and must open his mind to accepting new input. The longer the exchange continues, the more opportunities arise for modification or expansion of the original intent.

If a third party enters the process, we're playing a whole new ball game and additional factors must be considered. At what point in the transmissions did the third (or fourth or nth) party join? Has the newcomer been brought up to date and informed of the purpose of the interchange? How do this person's attitudes relate to or differ from those of the original communicators? In other words, is everybody tuned in on the same wavelength?

Receiver reaction can be affected in unexpected ways, and circumstances surrounding a written message but independent of either communicator can generate unexpected results. The example that comes to my mind involved a large business firm that used payroll stuffers—slips of paper in each pay envelope—to notify employees of special events, fringe benefits, and the like. Once the reproduction department asked payroll what color paper should be used for printing a particular message. Payroll responded that it didn't matter, so reproduction chose some surplus stock it wanted to use up. When the employees opened their

GUIDE TO WRITTEN COMMUNICATION

1. *Determine your purpose.*
   Even a personal letter has an objective (to send or ask for information, request action, extend an invitation, etc.).

2. *Plan the length.*
   Is the amount of reading required of your receiver appropriate and desirable? A personal letter to a close friend can be long; a business memo should be brief and to the point.

3. *Relate to the reader.*
   This influences your writing style and choice of words. When you are replying to a written communication, rereading it before putting your pen to paper strengthens your empathy.

4. *Write the communication.*

5. *Proofread the writing.*
   Sometimes intent isn't reflected in the finished product, or the overall message doesn't sound the same as the pieces did while being put together.

6. *Edit it.*
   A review and reworking aids clarity and impact.

Written communication can do the job it's intended to do if you do your job preparing it.

pay envelopes the following week, everyone received—of course, a pink slip. This color, unwittingly selected for practical reasons, transmitted a separate message (received humorously in this case) that had no relation to the printed words it contained.

Many factors are involved in written communication, and any one of them can detract from the effectiveness of our writing or even create a communication barrier. The brief Guide to Written Communication on the preceding page summarizes these factors in the framework of the structural steps outlined from the beginning of the chapter. If a writer builds his message solidly, then when he asks his receiver "Do you read me?" the answer will come back, "Loud and clear!"

5

PLAYING IT RIGHT

"When I tell my ten-year-old son to do something and he doesn't listen, I kick his ass! Is that what you need?"

So spoke the captain at a rifle range where I was in basic military training. The difficulty was that when I fell to the ground on command, my shoulders were forward of the chalked safety line. I knew I could correct the error by standing a little farther back than those to my left and right before dropping, but this wasn't permitted since I would have created an irregular starting position. Before I finally straightened up to fall right, the captain had made it very clear how he regarded both my performance and my status with him.

Several years (and status changes) later, I was invited to a business lunch by a top executive in an organization where I held a middle-management position. As we drove to the restaurant, he began to admire my automobile, which was in showroom-new condition though eight years old at the time. From the shining outside finish to the clean and well-preserved interior, my passenger praised one quality after another. Finally I said, "If you like the car so much, I'd be happy to hear an offer!" But my partner in conversation was to pull off both a topper and a consummate assertion of status. "I don't want to buy your car," he said in mock seriousness. "I'd like to have you clean up mine."

Between a rookie's standing with his commanding officer and a top executive's with his subordinate, there are infinite shadings and variations of the relative rank of communicators in each other's eyes. This chapter will examine some of them.

Establishing the relationship

During my senior year in college, I witnessed a masterful handling of status that I have never seen bettered. The practitioner was Dr. Milton Eisenhower, then not only president of my university but brother of the nation's president and thus a man whose high status drew instant recognition from anyone he communicated with. While I was in his office one day for a president-student interview, he placed a phone call to a department head to obtain some details and identified himself to the answering secretary, "Mr. Eisenhower calling." The significance of this phrasing didn't escape me. It would have been inappropriately unofficial for him to use only his first and last names, and referring to himself as "Dr." would have emphasized the discrepancy in rank between him and the staff member. Calling himself "Mr." reflected the intention to reduce that gap and create equality in the interchange—the act of a gracious man who obviously understood fully how differing status can affect dialog.

Establishing the relationship is something that all communicators do, whether deliberately or intuitively. I am not referring here to on-the-job status, which is largely fixed by the relative position of the communicators in the organization hierarchy. In transitory interchange, on the contrary, it must be worked out early in the contact. The ultimate success or failure of the transaction hinges on both whether this relationship is established and whether that status arrangement is accepted by both parties. The clerk in a store who is uncomfortable in a service role will display an attitude that will make customer satisfaction impossible. On the other hand, a shopper who approaches a clerk with condescension or an excess of assumed authority will trigger hostility and provoke your classic marketplace skirmish.

Status recognition is of course a function of a given communicator's identity and the esteem it enjoys (or doesn't enjoy) in the partner's value system. Thus mistaken identity can derail an exchange when two people maintain similar status standards, share the same intent in the exchange, and otherwise satisfy the rules for effective communication. An experience early in my adult life illustrates this.

After I had completed my military service, I embarked on a job search. My initial career plans lay in the area of writing for television. (In those days, the not-yet-vast wasteland hadn't expanded into an arid continent.) A friend of mine arranged an appointment with a New York advertising executive, a friend of his. This gentleman consumed little time on my qualifications and only enough minutes on job interests to bring forth my desire to write for television. Then he proceeded to lambaste that craft and berate its practitioners. His repeated reference to "you fellows" tied me in with those already employed in the industry. Following his tirade on the poor quality of TV writing and the sad state into which it was taking the new medium, he bid me an abrupt farewell. For several days I reflected on this misdirected communication, and I'm still not sure I know what happened.

Many prominent people set the stage for communication by identifying themselves. They're aware that in most cases, the knowledge of who they are will prompt people to give them immediate attention combined with a flatteringly deferential manner. When a well-known person must provide his or her own identification, it dampens the sender's satisfaction. Gregory Peck made this point vividly when he and a companion were waiting for a table in a restaurant. The other man, growing tired of the wait, asked Peck, "Why don't you tell them who you are?" To which the actor replied, "If you have to tell them who you are, you ain't!"

With collectives as with individuals, the name alone transmits an image as well as a central message. Try the following for impressions: Waldorf Astoria, Beverly Hilton, Chateau Frontenac, Mark Hopkins. Neighborhoods, business organizations, even hospitals communicate something merely through their names.

It's relatively safe to say that role status has the same impact in personal communication that it has in on-the-job exchanges. Instead of a superior-subordinate position, however, we're dealing with parent-child, hostess-guest, police-

man-citizen, captain–team member, or any one of dozens
of other roles we fill on a regular basis. It greatly aids communication if we consciously recognize our position in a
given interchange and assume the characteristics of our
status with regard to the other communicator(s) much as

Looking at it from your point of view,
what the hell does a dollar buy today?

an actor or actress adopts a part assigned in a play. Whether our approach is dominant or subordinate, cordial or restrained, more passive or more active, we must adjust our perspective to it. If we are unaware of our role in a given situation or refuse to accommodate it, this will do as much to impede discourse as a failure to practice all other requisites discussed in the preceding chapters.

Sensitivity to the role we have in a specific exchange does much to influence our level of attention and the appropriateness of our messages and responses. That is, the self-concept of each partner helps determine how much he commits himself to the communication process. Merely accepting a given status does little to guarantee meaningful discourse. Openness to communication is proportional to the ease and enthusiasm with which each party to it both lives his own role and accepts that of the other. An obstetrician's best audience is an expectant or hopeful parent.

Maneuvering for dominance

For every Dr. Eisenhower, underplaying his title and the status produced by it, there are countless people who squeeze every bit of mileage they can from forms of address denoting their rank in their field—judges, politicians, holders of advanced academic degrees. In this last group, I know a few who freely admit to having obtained a doctorate in part because they like the way Dr. sounds in front of their names. The advantage it generates in social settings is tantamount to virtually automatic communication dominance.

The late humorist and educator Stephen Leacock told a droll story on himself that illustrates the nonprofessional usefulness of a doctoral title. While he was on an ocean cruise, a fellow passenger fainted. The usual call for a doctor was sounded. When he saw how beautiful the collapsed woman was, Dr. Leacock's humanitarian instincts were immediately aroused. Although his degree was in jurisprudence, not medicine, he moved forward to see if he could be of some assistance. When he reached the patient, he found that he had already been preceded by two Ph.D.'s and a doctor of divinity.

There is a pecking order too among doctors dictated by the field in which the degree was taken. Historians seem to outrank sociologists, who in turn stand above, say, horticulturists. In American life, however, the medical doctor appears to be the king of the mountain (maybe because he earns the most money). I remember a young couple I knew slightly in my college years, the wife an M.D. and her husband a Ph.D. It was always interesting to me that most people assumed the husband to be the physician and his wife a college instructor, and he was frequently engaged in medical discussion or approached for advice. Perhaps in these days of increasing women's equality, people would be less inclined to commit such an error.

Dominance is established by many other earmarks besides a title, and these often originate from others rather than the person of distinction. Seating at a table and table assignment confer rank on an individual, whether the occasion is a social dinner, a wedding reception, or a business function. Those at the right of the host and hostess and at the head table enjoy special recognition and status. At large gatherings, prestige is also bestowed on people seated at the tables closest to the head table. These places are usually reserved for those receiving introductions or awards and for overflow from the head table. Status then decreases with distance from the head table. To overcome this arbitrary (and in many cases unintended) ranking, it is becoming common to dispense with a head table. The egalitarian effect of this is diminished to some degree, however, by the fact that the table where the principals are seated assumes dominance. In commercial establishments such as night clubs, theaters, and posh restaurants, we can buy our seating location.

The work we do and the organization we work for are determinants of our social status and hence of our relative position of dominance in any communication process. At a social gathering where all the guests aren't acquainted, note how frequently occupation is used to establish preferential treatment. It has always seemed to me that the question "What do you do for a living?" followed closely by "Where do you work?" constitutes as much an attempt by the inquirer to establish communicative status as to generate conversation. If the respondent provides answers that make the questioner feel dominant, the chances are strong for a prolonged and animated discussion.

A non-working wife may attempt to establish communicative dominance through her husband's position. Anyone who has served in the military knows the status enjoyed by, say, the colonel's wife, who couldn't command more prestige or exercise greater communication superiority if she herself wore the eagles. In business life, a wife or secretary takes for granted a dominance transferred from her husband or boss to herself and engages in communication from this vantage point. Women and men as well achieve status in communication also through their dress or the furnishings of their homes, as observed in

Chapter 3. Our place in line (or not having to stand in line at all), the promptness of others in keeping appointments with us, who speaks first, and dozens of other considerations act as signs of status and invariably affect our communication.

It would simplify matters considerably if we wore some insignia showing our occupation or our general niche in society similar to the designators of military rank. But this would have the undersirable effect of conditioning the participants before communication got under way and forcing it into a mold perhaps unrelated to the content of the message. Insofar as their identities allow, equality of communicators must govern any encounter that has the purpose of communication defined in the first chapter—an exchange of understanding. This egalitarianism is essential to effectiveness. If any significance at all is attached to the interchange, both (or all) parties should approach it in as flexible and open-minded a manner as possible. As the bromide states, if we don't know where we're going, we won't recognize the place when we get there. Yet the assumption must never be made that the road *we* travel is the only one to that destination.

One of our great fairway artists, Bobby Jones, compared life with the game of golf when he said, "You have to play it as it lays." To piggyback on this analogy, in good communication, you also have to play it right.

6

REACHING THOSE CLOSEST

The most rewarding results of applying everything we can learn about the art of communicating can come about right at home in the intimate environment of our family. Trying to understand how exchanges with loved ones get short-circuited not only generates harmony; it opens the door to some great surprises. One of my lessons was learned in front of a television set.

My daughter Susan has the practice of retaining the ballet costume that is specially ordered for her annual class recital. I'm sure all pupils in similar schools throughout the country do the same. The fact that each member of the group has the identical outfit has never made any kind of impression. It is rather the tradition of keeping the costume that has become vivid in her mind over the years.

One day as I sat watching some football on television, this ten-year-old entered the room and asked if it were a collegiate or professional game. The distinction had been explained to her on a previous occasion.

"Those are college players," I responded.

"What do they do when the game is finished?" she inquired.

"Why, they return to classes and study," I replied.

"Well," she followed, "do they get to keep their helmets?"

After this closing question, I realized what a difference in perspective can mean to family communication. The crux of successful transmission from a parent to a child or one spouse to the other is the ability to identify with the receiver's point of view. In the case of parent-child communication, an important element of this is adjustment to the child's plane of maturity and knowledge.

Avoid assumptions

Avoiding assumptions about the receiver's information, attitude, or memory in regard to a subject is a primary consideration in all family exchanges. In this connection, a little exercise I learned and used as an Air Force instructor provides a wry illustration of the inherent danger in making assumptions. In the military classroom, we would write *assume* on the blackboard. Then, breaking up the word and underlining the parts as we referred to them, we would say, "When you *assume* something, you make an *ass* of *u* and *me*."

With the exception of scientific communication concerning hypotheses, which by definition are assumptions, the sender and receiver should establish a common frame of reference before proceeding with an interchange. If simple, indisputable material is involved, it takes them only a brief moment to make certain that they are on the same wavelength. To state the obvious, the burden of this obligation lies with the parent in communication with a child. Words must be chosen for clarity, impact, and suitability to the receiver's level, as I said, and another family incident illustrates this point further.

A few years ago, my wife and our younger daughter were both ill, the latter only mildly, and were using different oral thermometers. One evening, M.A. directed our sick child to take her own temperature. "Don't use the thermometer in the solution," she called from her bed, referring to the fact that hers was standing in a container of supposedly sterilizing liquid. Unfamiliar with the word *solution*, Wendy picked up the wrong thermometer and placed it under her tongue. Within a few days, she came down with the more serious ailment—a casualty of both the virus and ineffective communication.

Susan's equation of a football helmet with her ballet costumes reflected a far subtler difference in backgrounds. She and I both recognized that the players required talent for their activity, that they had to practice, and that they were highly motivated. But that's where our shared frame of reference ended. I knew that this was only one of ten games on a team's schedule and not the most important, despite television coverage. I was also aware of the team's win-loss record and its ranking in college football over the years. But to my daughter, the contest was much more than a game. It was an annual recital, enhanced by being televised. She didn't have to understand the season's schedule or the team's status in the sport. Nor was she concerned that the players might need their helmets for other games. To her, this was a performance, for which they should be rewarded with a material memento.

Unless we understand and accept such interpretational differences, it is difficult if not impossible to evaluate messages or feedback correctly. In the instance of that football game, had Susan and I been discussing a play or general proceedings, I would have weighed anything she said against my knowledge of her perspective. But were I not acquainted with a conversation partner's exposure to the sport, I could not be sure how much common ground we had. Assumption can therefore mislead more readily when our vis-à-vis is unfamiliar to us.

A difference in the sex of the parent and child may compound the difficulty of aligning mental and emotional standpoints. The father, being unable to identify with a girl of *any* age, may find it hard to grasp his daughter's perspective on many subjects. Should he finally make the necessary adjustment to achieve this empathy, he must then be sure to upgrade his communications as the child matures. Of course, the familiar cry of "You men are all alike!" or "I'll just never understand women!" can undermine efforts to achieve psychological unison, frustrating the opposite number and leading eventually to destruction of the delicate links in communication.

To get back on the firmer ground of discrepancies in simple information, take the case of a child of seven who is just becoming familiar with number concepts. Does providing a weekly allowance of 50 cents generate an appreciation of the value of money? Can such a practice begin to develop an understanding of the cost of maintaining a household or even of purchasing food?

If we first relate the allowance to the price of something the child wants to buy and then compare that item with, say, half a pound of ground beef, we can begin to inculcate a sense of food costs. (Having already bought countless hamburgers from fast-food stands, our learner knows the price of ready-to-eat ground beef, which provides a basis for comparing do-it-yourself with prepared-and-served meals.) By quantifying the cost of an item in terms of what the child's allowance will buy, we've established a mutual point of departure, one that fits within the perspective of both. This is not only informative; it is courteous as well.

One episode in our family that was pleasant for the adults but had no meaning for the children points up the gap in understanding when perspectives differ. This event illustrates a child's frustration at being unable to share the reaction of the senior members. On one occasion, my mother bought some raffle tickets at a charity block party and wrote in the names of my two daughters. To the delight of the adults, four-year-old Wendy won second prize. Our enthusiasm was caught by the prize winner, and she gleefully jumped up and down. Finally she thought to ask what she had won. When told it was a basket of assorted wine, she looked puzzled. Then her surprise gave way to tears.

"What are you crying about" I asked.

"I don't even drink wine," she replied in complete confusion.

If it were only a matter of growing up, household communication would ultimately be trouble-free. But, alas, even people who have lived together for years get their wires crossed. One morning, my wife and I were discussing the dinner menu for guests who were coming that night. We agreed that we should serve a favorite type of roll, which was available from a local bakery. Late in the afternoon, I performed a regular household function of mine that is second only to my taking out the garbage—picking up the few odd grocery items needed between regular shopping trips. With my wife's list in hand, I departed. After my return, she asked me where the dinner rolls were. As my defense for having forgotten to buy them, I pleaded not guilty because rolls had not appeared on the list. My wife said she had taken them for granted, assuming our discussion had established that they should be included with the other purchases.

Nobody's a mind reader

Making assumptions about a partner in communication stands toe to toe with another ubiquitous gremlin in family relations: failure to inform. Volumes could be written regarding misunderstandings, crossed signals, and communication breakdowns that have occurred because one of the parties in an exchange didn't (or couldn't possibly) know certain facts or thoughts possessed by the other. What's more, these shortcomings continue to surround us at an increasing rate.

A not uncommon family example is the wife who has confirmed her pregnancy but hasn't yet decided how or when she'll inform the husband. All her conversation and attitudes are colored by this knowledge, but until her husband is tuned in on the situation, differing perspectives caused by the missing fact in his frame of reference prevent them from communicating realistically.

Or take the child who has broken a valuable vase while playing inside the house. Depending on how parental conditioning has affected his viewpoint on the seriousness of this accident, he may feel anything from mild worry to severe anxiety. Whatever his reaction, until he discloses what he has done, the parent will not be able to appraise requests or comments made by the child, all of which will be influenced by the destroyed item. "Are you still going to the school play on Saturday?" asks the offspring, trying to confirm a commitment made before the accident. "Yes, I think so," replies Mother, wondering why her child has asked the question.

Of course, parents usually interpret such clues very quickly, responding with appropriate questions to determine the cause of this doubt and insecurity. But the fact remains that until both parties to the discussion are in possession of the same information, they are spinning wheels.

A friend of mine and his family decided they would ride together to stay in stride together, building rapport and health through bicycles. The three teenage sons already had bikes, but the parents had to buy some for themselves. Dad selected a deluxe 12-speed European creation with all accessories. Mom acquired a more conventional model.

Because of the delicate equipment and special knowledge required to use the father's bike, the mother advised her sons not to touch it. However, she neglected to explain the reasons, which involved their safety. Thinking this blanket prohibition was prompted by selfishness on his dad's part, the youngest of the trio succumbed to temptation and took the fancy two-wheeler on a spin around the block.

As might be expected, the 13-year-old lost control going downhill. While turning to avoid a car, he ran over a curb and hung Daddy's pride on a large blossoming bush. Although the boy was only scratched and slightly shaken,

You men are all alike!   *I'll just never understand women.*

the bike looked like something from a junk dealer's going-out-of-business sale. If Mom's injunction had included the reasons, Dad's new toy might have been preserved.

Of course, disclosure has limitations where feelings rather than facts are involved, and utter frankness can cause problems in even the closest of families. Most of us have seen feuds develop because someone felt compelled to "tell it like it is." Therefore, the ability to reveal all the facts to others must be tempered by control of forthrightness, a skill that children (and some adults) have to learn.

It's rather common, for example, for a child to be totally direct when the youngster is discussing a third party.

"How's your daddy?" inquires a neighbor in extending a passing greeting.

"He's much better now," replies the child.

"What was the matter?" responds the neighbor, unaware that this routine salutation would produce discourse.

"Well, he's been home with the flu most of the week," continues the child.

"Bet that kept your mom busy," a reply designated to terminate the discussion.

"Yes, it did, and the doctor told her not to spend too much time on her feet."

"Why is that?" curiosity takes over.

"She's going to have a baby."

This sort of exchange, which leaves nothing to the imagination, is not unusual when a child is involved. However, when disclosure involves adults, we can expect that what's said has been filtered to strain potential emotional content. Sometimes, as in this next exchange, something fouls it up.

"Was the convention successful?" inquired a wife as she greeted her husband and his fellow salesman on their return from a three-day, out-of-town gathering.

"Never attended a better one," replied the spouse.

"Your husband's quite a dancer," added his companion.

"Oh, I didn't know you had time for social activity," challenged the wife.

"It wasn't exactly what you're thinking," protested the husband.

"What should I be thinking?" questioned the wife.

"Well, you see, one night everyone from our region went to dinner at this club," explained the husband. "They had a small band there, and some of the women in our group wanted to dance."

"I'm sure you all had a good time," said the wife.

"He's got a great sense of rhythm," interrupted hubby's companion.

"Good night, Walt," said the husband, ending the conversation and precluding additional disclosure.

This dialog, generated by disclosure on the part of the husband's companion, was basically open and innocent, but there are undertones and innuendos that no one really intended.

Static in the air

As we know, the core of a message (or of the feedback to it) may bear little resemblance to what shows on the surface. Nowhere is this truer than in the family, despite the depth of knowledge that its members generally have of each other. The main reason is the very intensity of the relationships, which heightens each person's expectation that the others can and will read minds. Sometimes they can. Often all that gets through to them is static, and it's usually emotional rather than mental.

It is difficult to understand a transmission at times when stress—negative or positive—alters customary patterns of communication. Can a wife, for instance, fully empathize with her husband's exhilaration on closing a big sale, which means not only earning a fat commission but acquiring the prestige reserved for the big boys? His thoughts, messages, and responses for days will be colored by the euphoria resulting from this success. Conversely, if her outlook shifts temporarily because she has landed an important new client, will he be able to appreciate concomitant changes in her viewpoints? If she forgets his birthday or doesn't recall his golf date for the weekend, can he fathom and accept this lapse of memory? Or in the event that continued success causes a permanent change of attitude in one, can the other accommodate and reach this altered personality by adjusting her or his own communication practices?

Children are likely to manifest markedly altered communication patterns as they enter adolescence. Much of their transmission will really concern the emotional upheavals of this troubled but blooming period in human life, whatever the surface messages. This is the time when the generation gap begins to intrude into family relations.

With all the publicity given to this rite of passage in the past decade, one could almost conclude that it is a recent phenomenon, produced by contemporary parental permissiveness. It takes only a brief perusal of social documentation to see that such a chasm has yawned between elders and youngers throughout history. Ancient Greek philosophers despaired of the alienation of youth from the ways of their seniors. And Alexander Pope, in his *Essay on Criticism*, wrote:

> *We think our fathers fools, so wise we grow;*
> *Our wiser sons, no doubt, will think us so.*

Every teenager thinks himself unique, an opinion reinforced by stronger peer support. But adults rather unfeelingly tend to categorize this age as a time of dreams and poor judgment. Quite obviously, these radically diverse perspectives can't be reconciled into a shared point of view. Throughout the teen years, the younger family member continues to have the more limited ability to project into another's point of view, in large measure because of less experience. It therefore behooves the parents to make the greater efforts to achieve a basis for communication. Of course, to regard a common perspective as all that is needed to close the generation gap would be simplistic nonsense. But it is the first step toward reestablishing a dialog that could yield an empathic exchange. Bringing about communication between a teenager and parents doesn't imply an end of the growth revolution but merely a truce that fosters understanding of a given issue on both sides. And that can significantly reduce the static.

Settled attitudes of one spouse toward the other may short-circuit a transmission just as thoroughly as underlying emotions will. For example, a husband who opposes his wife's shopping trips on principle will muster every weapon in his arsenal to express his disapproval (negative tone of voice, brusque manner, silently raised eyebrows) when she's setting off on one. Take this exchange between a pair who have recently moved to a new city:

WIFE   Can I get anything for you while I'm at the shopping center?

HUSBAND   There's nothing I really need, dear; and besides, you probably won't have any money left after *you* get through.

WIFE   Well, let me worry about that! Just say if you want something.

HUSBAND   What I really want is for you not to go shopping.

WIFE   That isn't gonna happen, honey, so I'll see you later.

HUSBAND   O.K., but you probably could have picked a less busy time of week to make the trip. The traffic is heavy on that route even during slow periods.

WIFE   Please tell me where to get off so I can avoid the interchange where everything usually gets backed up.

HUSBAND   I'd be happy to tell you where to get off, sweetheart, but on second thought, better go the long way. You'd probably pass the exit in all that traffic anyhow.

Not only has the husband made his point (repeatedly); he has made himself disagreeable at the same time. But his reluctance to communicate is unmistakable. His attitude has conveyed to his wife his displeasure with her shopping trip, as indeed her attitude has conveyed to him a determination to proceed.

One of the commoner causes of static in family communication is me-toomanship. This is the determination to have one's say, to provide input into all discussions and decisions. If a family is accustomed to accommodating every member's comments, this process can be fun, albeit as time-consuming as there are numbers of people in the household. In a large family or where individual input occurs at random—regardless of whether anyone else is speaking—we witness the onset of verbal pollution.

Since this more-the-merrier approach violates rule 2 of both sending and receiving, effective communication is drowned out. What we have instead is a conversational brawl. When the tumult subsides, some of the participants may wonder not only what happened but what they themselves said. Now, someone will surely comment that this is family give-and-take, with no real communication intended. Perhaps. But it establishes a pattern in both adults and children of casual and self-centered discussion. And it can certainly sow the seeds of poor communication practices in younger members of the group, even if it strengthens self-expression and develops individuality.

If a parent moderates mealtime conversation so as to keep this static down, the family can have the benefit of both individual participation and good training in communication skills. Like many other abilities, effective communication practices can be acquired at home.

7

TRYING TO DO A JOB

Professor Abraham Zaleznik of the Harvard Business School has stated a fundamental difficulty in achieving more effective communication in our jobs:

> Where one individual has the capacity to control and affect the actions of another . . . by virtue of differences in their positions, knowledge, or experience, then the feeling governing the relationship tends to be one of distance and (hopefully) respect, but not one ultimately of warmth and friendliness.*

Given this analysis, the greater the spread between two people on the organization ladder, the greater the difficulty in establishing the basic rapport necessary for communication. Even if one of the parties is an able communicator, the psychological distance between sender and receiver con-

* Abraham Zaleznik, "The Human Dilemmas of Leadership," *Harvard Business Review* (July-August 1963), p. 51.

stitutes an obstacle to mutual perspective. That is not the only impediment to transmission in a business firm; its very nature as an aggregate of people legislates against the efficiency that a one-to-one exchange can have. But in a concern of any size, excepting sometimes partnerships, the necessary superior-subordinate structure builds in a pervasive communications damper. The problem can be sorely exacerbated if the big fish also have big egos.

Status jockeys and how they ride

My first real exposure to the hobbyhorse of ego in business occurred during a summer of my college years that I spent working as a busboy. The captain of the busboys wasn't a three-month employee like the rest of us; he worked at this job on a year-round basis—it was his career. He stood 6 feet 4, boasted a muscular frame, and was very proud of his title and responsibility but none too fond of the summer troops. The students for their part didn't think much of this boss, who performed such menial work for a livelihood and from whom they were required to take orders.

One weekend, it was necessary to reset the entire dining room before dinner with only two hours' notice. In a departure from his usual procedure, our captain called no group meeting, deciding instead to work directly with each busboy. With this procedure, he had it both ways, leaning heavily on those who goofed—"What's the matter, college boy, don't they teach you how to take orders at school?" —while goading those who succeeded into correcting others' mistakes: "O.K., bright boy, so you understand English! Now go explain the language to your slower buddies." He was apparently oblivious to the contempt in which we held his vanity, a reaction that precluded any rapport between him and us.

We busboys, countermotivated to resetting the dining room, maliciously (if perhaps subconsciously) determined to embarrass the captain. It was this goal toward which we all channeled our effort. Not surprisingly, disaster struck— a simple task became a summer-resort Waterloo. Almost everyone's section was improperly set up, no extra hands were available to correct the errors, and time didn't permit us a second effort. Some of the vanity displayed in this episode obviously came from the busboys as well, through their better-than-thou attitude. The net effect was that the message from the captain not only got no valid feedback but generated the opposite result of what he had intended. Dinner was a little late that night.

Numerous subsequent experiences underlined the influence that ego has on communication. In a firm I worked for some years ago, subordinates were not merely inhibited but visibly fearful in the presence of the chief executive. One afternoon I wanted to introduce someone from outside the organization to the boss. As I entered the top man's office to inquire if he would meet this person, he was getting into his coat for an early departure. "Are you leaving for the day?" I inquired.

The shock of my forwardness elicited a nonverbal put-down, consisting in his lowering his head while peering at me over the top of his eyeglasses. Then realizing that my inquiry had purpose, he asked, "Why? Is there something you want me for?" I briefed him, whereupon he requested a minute to get ready for the visitor. After he phoned, I ushered the guest in to meet him.

As we entered the first-class office of the No. 1 man, I

was surprised to find him seated at his desk busily scanning a report. He did not look up following my introduction but waited for the visitor to speak first. Besides fitting the role he played, his action also accommodated his strategy of putting others on the defensive and thus grasping the dominant position in the communication that would follow. To leave no doubt about the authoritarian style he chose to use, this executive often boasted that he didn't get ulcers—he gave them.

Ego strutting isn't limited, of course, to top-level people in business; in fact, the most frenetic status competition probably occurs among middle managers who are close to equal in the organization hierarchy. Here the inroads of self-absorption are likely to take a great toll in performance. Two people who are busy determining which one should be deferential or dominant cannot maintain the necessary objectivity in the important task of communicating. Moreover, when one has gained the superior position, that communicator is then likely to pursue his ego trip, and there's simply no room for such psychological joy rides in good communication practices. The height of pompousness is the imprinted heading on a manager's memo paper, "*From the desk of* ____" An exchange of memos on such paper results in the ludicrous situation where we have two desks communicating with each other.

"Every bird loves to hear himself sing," goes a German proverb, and men are no less fascinated with their own pronouncements. Some even feel that, if they're doing the talking, it's coming directly off the hot line. Conveying urgency obtains greater concentration from the receiver, which increases the likelihood that the message will be understood accurately. However, there are those who make every business communication sound like an invasion from outer space. An executive acquaintance of mine always generated immediacy by the tone and volume of his voice even when ordering a cup of coffee, thereby earning himself the nickname "Huff-and-Puff." In cumulative effect, this boy-who-cried-wolf delivery tends to create lackadaisical recipients by making it difficult for them to perceive and react to priorities. Ultimately it produces condescension from others rather than the alert and responsive attitude it was designed to stimulate.

Hearing what you want to hear

Besides the psychological impasses created by a sender's job level or posturing, the receiver's predispositions can scramble the content of a message. We've all heard success stories based on the contrary—the heightened impact a transmission had on the boss or a coworker because he was in "a good mood." So it comes as no surprise that anticipation in business communication can lead a receiver to hear the message that he wants to hear. There is the popular anecdote about a business owner charging his manager with responsibility for the concern before going off on a lengthy vacation. "Treat this company as though it were your own," said the boss. Within two weeks the manager sold the place. The receiver's attitude had dramatically conditioned his interpretation of the message and hence his response.

Perspectives differ especially often in business communication and must be aligned if sending and receiving are to be effective. The following dialog gives another illustration of divergence between intent and interpretation. Note

that the actual words spoken are for the most part innoc-
uous—a succession of almost meaningless comments and
observations. But given the recipient's expectations, the
transmission, though obviously not designed to generate
misunderstanding, does the job as well as if it had been
planned by experts.

The scenario is a performance review and it features
the president of a small firm and a manager whose work is
unsatisfactory. The president knows how to conduct such
job critiques. First, he'll mention the strong points of this
subordinate's work to bolster his ego and pave the way for
criticism. Next, he'll cover shortcomings. He'll then provide challenge and a look ahead to close on a positive note.
However, the end result isn't what's called for in the script,
as we'll see. Here is the exchange itself:

PRESIDENT: Your work isn't bad, Roger.
      (Intent: It's adequate to get you by.)
      (Roger's interpretation: I do a good job.)
ROGER: Well, I certainly try hard enough.
      (Intent: My efforts and ability account for the good
      work.)
      (President's interpretation: Ah, so it's the best you
      can do.)
PRESIDENT: You're people-oriented—sensitive to the needs
      of subordinates.
      (Intent: At least you get along with those in your
      department.)
      (Roger's interpretation: I'm a highly successful
      manager in the human relations area.)
PRESIDENT: However, your administrative work could
      use improvement.

(Intent: You're poorly organized, need to manage your time better.)

(Roger's interpretation: Ah, you're still upset about that report I turned in late.)

PRESIDENT: And you could work on cooperating with peers more fully.

(Intent: You must learn to get along with fellow managers.)

(Roger's interpretation: You're aware of my lead-the-pack performance, that ability to move out in front.)

ROGER: I appreciate what you're saying.

(Intent: Obviously you value my kind of approach.)

(President's interpretation: You're getting the message.)

PRESIDENT: I'm going to give you a special assignment, Roger.

(Intent: Here's a chance to redeem yourself, to get back on the right track.)

(Roger's interpretation: It's a test for better things. You want me to prove how good I really am.)

PRESIDENT: Properly handled, it could lead up the ladder.

(Intent: If this is done well, it will put you back in our good graces, maybe even result in future advancement.)

(Roger's interpretation: I'm due for promotion!)

PRESIDENT: This is important for you, Roger.

(Intent: Otherwise you're on the way out.)

(Roger's interpretation: I'm on the way up!)

That evening, Roger tells his wife, "The boss and I had a talk today. He told me I'm getting promoted soon." And shortly everybody in the firm knows who's being groomed for vice-president.

Managerial options

Some managers keep coming up short despite well-intentioned efforts. One reason may be the barricades set up by the prerogatives of the job itself. The fact that a manager has access to a preferred parking spot, or that he customarily eats in the executives' dining room, is bound to influence his discussions about the company parking lot and the cafeteria. Ability to regulate thermostat controls certainly affects what a person has to say about the comfort of his work zone.

Other obstacles to good communication are generated by a manager's work habits. Take for example a reluctance to handle the telephone until a connection has been made. Somewhere between Peter Drucker's time-management suggestion to avoid placing and receiving calls directly and Robert Townsend's injunction to dial it yourself, every business person must find a middle road that makes for personal efficiency in communicating. Just as face-to-face contact provides a sender with the feedback nuances that are otherwise unavailable, handling the phone, mail, or the drop-by visitor directly on occasion will broaden one's overall communication perspective. When one's view becomes too broad, however, other choices may influence the fine art of exchange. The hazards of full disclosure were illustrated in Chapter 6.

At the other extreme, there's the practice of being misleading in communication. Such tactics are wasteful at the very least. Like one who attempts to pour a gallon into a quart, the equivocator spills words indiscriminately for the purpose of filling a defined need. Some people equivocate to keep all the doors open, and some do it to deceive. Equivocation in fact detours communication and cuts the receiver off. Some managers are gifted in the art of waffling. The following exchange is familiar to all of us, because every organization has someone like the boss—

Miss Johnson, I have a message of great importance for all employees. Please connect me with the grapevine.

who is guilty of drawing unjustified inferences—and the manager—who is guilty of permitting him to.

"That's a great plan," said the manager's boss after examining it. "Could fill our need for Chicago as well as Kansas City."

"Exactly what I had in mind," added the manager (who hadn't evaluated its use for either city).

"Think it would be applicable two years from now?" asked the boss.

"Don't know why not," answered the manager (who didn't know why, either). Taking the cue from his superior, he continued, "My original thinking was to make it as flexible and multifaceted as possible, capable of being utilized in several cities over an extended period of time."

"It certainly has a variety of applications," added the boss.

"That's by design, of course," concluded its proud creator as he wrapped up his exercise in snowmaking.

Then there are managers who are accomplished at avoiding commitment. "Haven't had time to study it," or "As soon as I've had a chance to digest it, we'll get together" reflects evasion of communication. Often, the conversation following that digestion strays far from target. In a flat-out indictment of his colleagues, the vice-president of one of the country's largest business organizations recently said, "American executives talk too much and have an uncanny ability to evade the point." Sometimes it's a desire to have things both ways. This brings to mind some stories about a famous athletic manager, Frank Leahy. When Leahy was head football coach at Boston College before moving on to sports immortality at Notre Dame, he had a sign in the locker room that read:

RULES
1. *The coach is always right.*
2. *If the coach is wrong, see rule 1.*

As was his custom, Leahy predicted the worst when he took his team to New Orleans to play Tulane. "How can we be expected to win? They're training and practicing while our muscles are getting stiff from the train ride." But when hosting an out-of-town team that had to make a long trip to Boston, Leahy said "How can we be expected to win? We're getting tired from so much practice while they're fresh and rested from the long train ride."

Certainly, there is always the option which says something by doing nothing—inaction. This comment appeared recently in a business magazine article:

> Some VPs, in fact, admit they are now doing everything they can to keep out of the line of fire. One financial vice-president at a Texas machine-tool company, for example, candidly says that he is hedging his actions and decisions every time he figures he can get away with it. "I'm not especially proud of it," he states, "but playing it safe is just about the only way I can save myself from getting into deep trouble." *

Pass the word

In many situations communication is beyond our individual control, if not out of our hands. The middlemen who enter the picture are as common in business communication as they are in the marketplace. Sometimes they are recognizable, but mostly they function as silent partners in confusion.

---

* Thomas J. Murray, "Industry's Disenchanted VPs," *Dun's* (November 1974), p. 78.

Although informal, incomplete, and certainly unofficial, a company's grapevine is probably its fastest and most popular communication system. Many view it as a gossip channel, but this discounts the fertile soil of fact in which it grows. Some grapevines have limited spread, involving only a department or several areas in proximity, while others extend throughout an entire organization, reaching even its most remote geographical locations.

Since the grapevine is here to stay, let's assess its operation and communicative function briefly. First, such a network is not just an idle medium of diversion for employees. It serves a positive purpose by permitting people to talk about events in their life at work, which is a proven psychological need, and it satisfies the desire to be "in on things," a factor repeatedly rated high in surveys of what workers consider important to morale. Second, because we all like talking about things that affect us or are familiar, the grapevine can supply the most rapid and most powerful route for information spread within a company.

Many organizations, aware of the grapevine's importance, intentionally leak items into it to inform employees or to counter some unfavorable story currently making the rounds. This is effective on-the-job transmission. In some instances, the grapevine may strengthen formal communication or add a perspective that can't be conveyed through official channels. It's possible, too, for a grapevine to raise employees' expectations or color their attitudes to the point where management is required to respond to pressures generated by it, but this would be a deviation from the grapevine's usual role. Research conducted by Professor Keith Davis, of Arizona State University, indicates that in normal operation, between 75 and 95 percent of grapevine information is correct though incomplete.

Whenever I think of the possible 25 percent inaccuracy, I'm reminded of a friend who survived the dissolution of his entire department. Some of his former colleagues were transferred to other areas, and several were fired. On the day following this bombshell, my friend was approached in the company cafeteria by an associate who said, "Boy, am I glad to see you!" "Why?" asked my friend. "Do I owe you money?" "No," replied the other fellow, "but word has it you are no longer with us." In the absence of an official announcement, which was still in preparation, the grapevine immediately filled the vacuum with not altogether accurate information. That afternoon, following several similar encounters, my friend answered the phone to hear a caller from a distant office of the organization report the same rumor. At this point, he said, he could only paraphrase Mark Twain by responding that reports of his demise were premature.

When chain communication extends outside an organization, the chances for inaccuracy expand geometrically. As a case in point, take conventions and large group meetings, a realm where Murphy's Law is always operative: If anything can go wrong, it will. One reason is the many details that go into a finished program, but a more important consideration from the standpoint of communication is the number of people involved.

It's a truism that the accuracy of a message decreases as the number involved in relaying it increases. This has been demonstrated in several recent television talk shows, but it's an effect long recognized and variously illustrated by wits in the business world. Operation Halley's Comet is an amusing illustration. In fact, since it is impossible to locate the original source of the story, it may even have been subject to the same transmogrifications it illustrates:

Operation Halley's Comet

Colonel to Executive Officer: Tomorrow evening at approximately 2000 hours, Halley's Comet will be visible in this area, an event which occurs only once every 75 years. Have the men fall out in the battalion area in fatigues, and I will explain this rare phenomenon to them. In case of rain, we will not be able to see anything, so assemble the men in the theater and I will show them films on it.

Executive Officer to Company Commander: By order of the Colonel, tomorrow at 2000 hours, Halley's Comet will appear above the battalion area. If it rains, fall the men out in fatigues, then march to the theater where this rare phenomenon will take place, something which occurs only once every 75 years.

Company Commander to Lieutenant: By order of the Colonel, the phenomenal Halley's Comet will appear in the theater in fatigues at 2000 hours tomorrow evening. In case of rain in the battalion area, the Colonel will give another order, something which occurs once every 75 years.

Lieutenant to Sergeant: Tomorrow at 2000 hours, the Colonel will appear in the theater with the phenomenal Halley's Comet in fatigues, something which happens every 75 years. If it rains, the Colonel will order the comet into the battalion area.

Sergeant to Squad: When it rains tomorrow at 2000 hours, the phenomenal 75-year-old General Halley, accompanied by the Colonel, will drive his Comet through the battalion area theater in fatigues.

A slightly stretched example of course, but it illustrates what happens: As individuals pass a message along a line, it is modified at each link in the transmission chain. When it reaches the end, it has gotten not only highly but ludicrously distorted. This is merely an extrapolation from the "But he said" and "I thought you meant" misunderstandings that enter into the complex task of getting across. Beware the middle man! In communication, three may not be a crowd, but it's the beginning of chaos.

Once when I was running a seminar for 50 participants, I told the hotel program coordinator (an employee of ours) that the faculty would require several large blackboards, some corkboards for tacking up charts, and other materials. On inspecting the seminar site several weeks later just before the event, I found one large blackboard and several corkboards. The maintenance supervisor, whose group had actually set up the room, wanted to know if the green corkboards were satisfactory since they had none in black.

In tracking the communication breakdown, I learned that my request to our company program coordinator went to the hotel salesman handling our account, who conveyed it to the function manager, who relayed it to the maintenance supervisor. Nowhere in this communication chain was there an understanding of the importance of blackboards to the presentations. Then there was the matter of trying to maintain a satisfactory room temperature during the program, but that's another story!

There are two ways for the organizational message sender to prevent disaster from this type of foulup: (1) to obtain feedback from each link in the chain of transmission, or (2) to inspect the end product so as to detect errors. To the question "Must total feedback always be obtained?" I would answer by asking, "How important is the reason for communicating?"

Even when the requirements have been planned carefully and communicated effectively, it's not always possible to avoid difficulty. I recall one seminar conducted out of town for which the president of our company flew in especially to make an appearance. I was in charge of things. Opening the morning's agenda, he remarked in passing that his room had not been made up on his arrival late the previous night. After this comment, a friend looked at me and raised his index finger to indicate one strike. Then the president stated how happy he was to be there, even though nobody had informed him which room in this very large hotel was assigned for our meeting. My friend again glanced in my direction and held up his index finger and thumb: strike 2. A few minutes later, while the president was making an important point, a stage phone directly behind him started ringing. Of course, he interrupted his remarks long enough to answer it, and my friend added his middle digit to the thumb and forefinger indicating I was out.

The grapevine, which gives us random multiperson communication, moves along a chain of transmission which may or may not be vulnerable at any of its many links. But the world of the committee is something else again, and the messages issued by such groups, whether appointed or self-designated, have a different set of problems. Of all the indictments leveled at the committee, perhaps the most damaging is that it is ineffective. Certainly the commonest charge made is that it consumes excessive time in performing its task, but questioning its reason for existence does damage to the very word.

Now, anyone who has ever served on a committee knows it can't be all bad. After all, here is the opportunity to exchange opinions, to persuade others of our point of view, to obtain consensus, and to generate a feeling of achievement. Alas, the failure of the committee is directly related to its inability to communicate. Every factor that contributes to short circuits in interpersonal exchange is amplified in group transmission. It compounds the failure of individual communication.

First, the committee combines into one unit people with diverse educational backgrounds, lifestyles, perspectives, and job objectives. The greater the number of members, the smaller the chance for common understanding. That is, effective communication is inversely proportional to the size of the group. When the decision or program under consideration is a difficult one, the chance of success is reduced further yet. Even the most skilled chairman cannot guarantee that the message will be received the same way by all participants let alone reconcile their various interpretations of it. Once the facts themselves are subject to disagreement, progress based on these facts becomes impossible. In addition, the members' reactions, comments, and behavior provide secondary considerations and tend to derail the real purpose of the conference.

It was once my wearying duty to appear before a committee convened to determine which executives in the organization would be entitled to a company car. After meeting two hours a week for eight weeks, the group reached its decision. A few days later, every member of that committee was driving a newly leased company automobile.

Another group I participated in was charged with determining policy on employee insurance. Various outside agents were invited to make presentations and answer the committee's questions. Finally, several months later, time came to develop a program. Although everyone had sat through the same proceedings, no two agreed on the meaning of what had been said over the weeks, much less on how it applied to employee needs or the group's effort. Our chairman then disbanded his committee and, with management's blessing, turned its responsibility over to the personnel department.

For any committee to succeed, the group must be small, fast-paced, and dedicated to its own dissolution. Only by rapidly accomplishing its set tasks will it be able to communicate its conclusions and justify its original creation.

In any setting where we communicate, developing an awareness of that environment provides valuable guidance for both sending and receiving. At work, it is particularly important to discern whether it is appropriate in terms of self-interest to be involved in any given transmission. Like a third party to a private conversation or fight, we can find ourselves inadvertently intruding or being drawn into a situation where we had no place. On the other hand, reluctance to participate can make us miss input that is necessary or helpful for our performance or on-the-job relationships. Once we decide how far we should be involved, we can then bring our communication skills into play to derive maximum benefit from the encounter.

8

BEING TAKEN, SERIOUSLY!

"Two three-minute eggs, please."

After giving my order to the busy counter waitress, I started to read a morning newspaper. Soon a plate was placed before me with two fried eggs on it.

"These aren't three-minute eggs," I protested.

"Look, mister," came the curt response, "the cook is too busy to time everyone's egg order."

So it goes. The farther we move from spheres of the familiar—immediate family, social friends and acquaintances, business colleagues, everyday store personnel—the more incidents of communication failure beset us. Although the reasons for inaccuracy vary widely, the results are the same: an incorrect or unsatisfactory transaction—or none at all.

Quasi-communication

An inability or unwillingness to fathom a sender's intent is often the wrench in the communication works, and it ac-

counts for more serious problems than an error at a break-
fast counter. For example, when we purchased our home
several years ago, the builder agreed in writing to provide
basic landscaping to finish the grounds around the house.
On occasion I tried to discuss this matter with him, wanting
to know his plans and to share my thinking with him.
Whenever I brought up the subject, however, the builder
became disturbed and noncommittal. Finally, as the day of
the landscaper's arrival approached, I decided I had to pin
him down to specifics.

"Exactly what's going to be done to the property?" I
inquired.

His reply demonstrated his irritation. "Listen," he said
(using a word that was meaningless to him), "I'm not going to create the Garden of Eden in your backyard, that's
for sure."

In reality, I was more concerned with the practical consideration of water drainage away from the house than
with the appearance of my property. But any attempt to
get clarification was doomed. The builder seemed to feel
I was trying to pressure him into additional expense. He
stubbornly maintained his perspective, even criticizing himself for permitting us to occupy the home before it was
completely finished.

Less than a year after we had moved in, I entered our
basement one morning during the spring thaw and found
several inches of water covering the entire floor. Subsequent contact with our builder and our attorney led to the
courthouse. Since our sales agreement contained a one-year
guarantee of a dry basement, we were awarded reimburse-
ment for expenses we had incurred in relandscaping to correct the problem drainage.

Could effective dialog have nipped this situation in the bud? Could it have prevented that day in court? Such questions are academic, because the answers presume that the sender would have been willing to communicate his intent and his perspective as well as be receptive to the actions mandated by the interchange. It's my contention that such people see and hear only what fits their viewpoint. Instead of attempting to find enlightenment and clarification, they seek only justification for their preconceived objective, which in turn vindicates their actions. This creates a vicious cycle, where one party can't come out right because the other was never wrong in the first place. Just as nature requires a proper environment for growth, communication demands the fertility of open-mindedness.

Correcting our drainage problem provided still another example of missing pieces due to a sender's not communicating his intent and perspective to his receiver. The contractor I hired to install the necessary piping, regrade our yard, and restore surface landscaping furnished an estimate before performing the work. Although his figure was high, he said this was merely to cover unexpected costs and prepare me for the worst. The real bill, he indicated, would be for actual expenses and should total considerably less than his estimate. When the work was completed and the bill arrived, the amount charged was exactly the figure given in the estimate. Had this sum become familiar to him because of our several discussions of the estimate, or had he intended to ask that price from the beginning? At any rate, our subsequent discourse enabled us to reach a more acceptable total (for me at least), though it confirmed the fragile nature of even carefully specified oral agreements.

On the subject of costs, I'm reminded of a time I fell

victim to error in interpreting an incoming advertising message. The sign in front of a new steak house read, "You'll be surprised at our prices." Always interested in exploring an inexpensive taste treat, I took the family there for dinner. I was indeed surprised at the prices—unpleasantly so. Of course, the statement made no mention of what type of astonishment awaited the arrival of the check, in addition to which the cost of anything is relative and subject to individual attitude. The entire field of advertising communication, however, requires the receiver to be especially alert to the possibilities of misinterpretation.

Different frames of reference can bog down communication even when different intentions are perfectly clear. To illustrate, when a prospective customer visits a car dealer, he brings a desire to buy and some preconceived guidelines along. The salesman for his part has techniques for overcoming objections and all the information a buyer may require. What's missing, however—and destined to cause an immediate problem and possible future repercussions—is the presence of common reference. That "guarantee" described by our salesman in response to an anticipated customer inquiry is still often undefined and subject to interpretation, despite government and industry efforts in recent years to firm up the terms. The customer's limited understanding of warranty language, coupled with those inevitable assumptions he'll make, gives him less grasp of this part of the sales agreement than the salesman has, being exposed to its meaning on a routine basis.

Then there are the shifts in standard procedures as well as terminology that must be dealt with by a family relocating to another state, a rather common event in today's mobile society. When some friends of ours bought their first house in a Long Island community, they were represented by an attorney, who suggested that they purchase title-search insurance before "closing" the purchase. This established their frame of reference in home buying. When the husband changed jobs, they moved to suburban Boston, where they again retained an attorney to handle the "passing of papers." However, no title insurance was needed or suggested because there it was the responsibility of the bank's attorney, who searched the title and would not approve the sale unless that title was clear. Years later, in moving to Houston, the family discovered that titles there were the legal responsibility of the seller and many homes are bought without a lawyer's advice. Established perspectives do not accommodate changing conditions and must be modified if a receiver is to understand a message.

In any situation where the frame of reference is unknown or unusual, the first thing to do is to try to find a shared point of departure. This requires that both parties recognize the gap and sincerely want to narrow it. Then they can proceed to define terms, always maintaining sensitivity to possible misunderstanding and comprehension of and respect for the other's viewpoint. All these considerations are important in implementing meaningful communication.

Noncommunication

Noncommunication, like kinesics, is subject to a variety of interpretations. In body language, however, though the psychological state of the receiver may indeed color his perception of the nonverbal expression, the sender can exert much control over these influences to orient the receiver toward the intent of the message. One key, of course, is the sender's awareness of how silent transmission can affect the other communicator. A common example is two possible impressions conveyed when a person looks at a wristwatch. Is it a sudden recollection of a necessary activity (taking medication, placing a phone call), or does it reflect boredom? Only the sender really knows, but the manner and timing of the glance downward can reveal or conceal the true meaning of this action. Control is retained by an informed sender in either case.

Noncommunication occurs when an ongoing exchange, no matter how sporadic, ceases for long enough to make the partners in the exchange aware of it. It is a broader category than silence during a verbal exchange in that it includes unintentional omissions; silence is a conscious lapse. Silence in itself can take many forms, ranging from the expectant waiting of an employment interviewer who wants unstructured responses from an applicant to the put-down of a parent showing a child that a question isn't worth a reply.

Other kinds of noncommunication do transmit messages, but these are far more open to interpretation. One of my more obvious experiences with noncommunication occurred during a family vacation tour of Canada's Quebec Province. We stopped for lunch at a small establishment, and a young waitress approached to take our order. As soon as I began speaking, she turned abruptly and walked away, making a remark to another employee in French, which none of my family speaks. The second waitress then came to take our order.

Although this part of Canada is predominantly French-speaking, younger citizens are truly bilingual, conversing in French and English with a fluency that evokes both admiration and envy from less-gifted tourists. However, in this out-of-the-way location, our first waitress may have lacked that facility. On the other hand, if the personnel in the restaurant also had kitchen responsibilities, she may have remembered a pot boiling on the stove. Or she may have promised the second waitress a chance to practice English with the next English-speaking customers who came in, or she may have had a sudden fit of impatience. All I can say for certain is that she quickly conveyed her refusal to communicate for reasons that we never discovered.

Noncommunication may occur when one of the parties involved is a willing but ineffective participant because of a limited knowledge of the subject or inadequate empathy. Although poor listening habits may be at fault, the commoner cause is a sender-receiver mismatch. Thus absence of rapport can be attributed to disparate perspectives stemming from differences in age, sex, education, work experience, or economic status. Dialog difficulties between child and adult, husband and wife, intellectual and illiterate, and unionist and entrepreneur serve to illustrate this point. These are broad-scale divergences; the gap is often a good deal subtler.

Take a feud between previously good neighbors, or the breakup of a long friendship such as that of two young men whom we'll call Jack and Sid. This pair had established a strong bond during military service on the basis of similar interests, post-service career aspirations, and most of all a shared sense of humor. After their army days were over, Sid and Jack kept in touch. They even managed to visit each other twice, though they lived thousands of miles apart.

In one of his letters, Jack spoke of an opening that was

coming up in his company and suggested that Sid might be interested in it. If so, Jack said, he would get additional details and put his organization's employment manager in touch with his friend. Sid replied that he'd like to know more about the available position.

Before many weeks had passed, he received a phone call from a man who identified himself as an employment representative of Jack's company. He said he was in town on other business but would like to see Sid if possible. They had a pleasant meeting, during which Sid learned more about the company and its opening. Now fully informed

In case you're listening, I'm not speaking to you.

on the job, he decided he wasn't interested in it and indicated this to the interviewer.

In a letter to Jack written soon after this meeting, Sid thanked his friend for arranging the contact and explained his lack of interest. When several months passed without a reply, Sid wrote once more. But he never heard from his old buddy again.

An inquest on the abrupt demise of this strong friendship revealed several causes. First of all, Jack interpreted Sid's initial response as an indication of real interest and thus arranged for a recruiter to contact him instead of providing additional details. Letting enthusiasm get the better of him, Jack gave his friend a glowing buildup, implying that Sid was already interested in joining the firm. It was surprising then for the recruiter to find a man with a less-than-positive attitude toward the position who disavowed any further interest after receiving full information about it.

When told of the meeting, Jack was confused and slightly embarrassed. He had thought he was both helping his friend and strengthening their friendship. Because his employer was so successful and well known, it had never entered his mind that anyone might turn down an opportunity to take a job there. In addition to all this, the employment representative gave Jack some good-natured chiding about being off in the appraisal of his friend's intentions. It was a powerful combination of events that brought an end to a good friendship.

Now for the big ifs. Had the relationship between Jack and Sid involved a better understanding of each other, had they also communicated more fully in their correspondence, and had Jack's injured pride not created an imagined loss of status, another conclusion could have been written to their story. Given these lacunae, noncommunication took its toll in permanent alienation.

The foundations of an estrangement may not be so readily discoverable as the stumbling blocks that felled Jack and Sid's friendship. A case in point concerns two sisters who lived in different states and saw each other very infrequently. In fact, were it not for family social gatherings, they would probably not have visited with each other at all. When they did, it was clear that they didn't get along together.

Their daughters, who were friendly cousins, decided that some effort should be made to bring the women closer. Without attempting to find the cause of the friction, the daughters set about arranging meetings. Both mothers, however, always found reasons for being unable to keep the scheduled appointments and appeared uncomfortable about seeing one another.

Finally the cousins determined that they had to uncover the root of the problem. They agreed that each would ask her own mother why she didn't get along with the sister. Then they would compare the answers to see whether they could heal the breach. To their amazement, neither mother had an explanation for her attitude toward her sister, though both admitted that it had existed since they had been children. Unknown reasons had prevented each of them from initiating a discussion that would resolve their imagined conflict, which had seemed to intensify by feeding on itself.

Through the persistent efforts of their daughters, the sisters spent their older years enjoying the association and companionship they had deprived themselves of so long. Here an unexplainable avoidance of communication was at the bottom of a feud.

Supercommunication

At the opposite pole from the estranged sisters is a rare bird whom I call the supercommunicator. This is not the person who simply talks too much, for garrulity does not guarantee clarity and may indeed enshroud the message in such a mist of words that neither its surface nor its core is perceptible. This is the sender whose command of clear transmission is nigh on perfect but whose excessive attention to getting across can result in communication underkill. That is, the receiver has no difficulty understanding the message correctly but may be left with an impression that its originator is abrupt (at best) and frosty (at worst).

Like other perfectionists, the supercommunicator becomes harder to cope with the less the receiver knows of the whole person. A spouse or child may be annoyed by such a sender's method of transmission but will not find it an obstacle to rapport. Business associates will ordinarily take it in good spirit and may even consider it estimable. But in the uninitiate, the degree of exactitude and the ways it is pursued can produce something like a state of shock.

When speaking or writing, all supercommunicators select their words with great care. In regard to the content of the transmission, the fraternity divides into two main groups: those who expect the receiver to comprehend the message as delivered—devil take the hindmost who don't; and those who repeat unnecessarily and seek excessive feedback as assurance that they have gotten across. Both types can be guilty of talking down to an unknown receiver to avert the possibility of not being understood.

Overly efficient communicators conduct short, to-the-point conversations that open them to charges of anti-sociableness. Their tolerance for small talk is virtually nil; they tend to show impatience readily. They indulge nothing that won't contribute to message transmission or comprehension. Unlike the seasoned actor, who recognizes that every performance is a first for those who haven't seen it, a supercommunicator's lack of interest even in his own output increases with each repetition. Getting there (the first time) may have been half the fun, but being there twice is an outright bore.

At a social gathering, supercommunicators move freely but quickly among the others present, smiling, perhaps speaking briefly, then moving on. They usually like what they're drinking better than what they're hearing (which was W. C. Fields's reply to his mythical doctor when told that alcohol was affecting his auditory nerves). Committee meetings—business or other—are anathema to supercommunicators because they recognize the inherent barriers to effective interchange and the colossal loss of time involved. In fact, they are often time conservationists, frequently consulting the clock and strictly budgeting the hours in a day.

When the supercommunicator takes pen in hand, it is usually for a brief memo or a quick letter. His approach has altered the familiar bromide to read: If it's worth writing at all it's worth writing briefly. Pompous writing style drives him to destruction of his ballpoint.

Routinely avoiding a paragraph if he can say it in a sentence, he sometimes omits pertinent information, and if he falls into this trap often enough he will fail to achieve productive interchange. The supercommunicators must join the others we've discussed in this chapter and attempt improvement. Perhaps they can start by being less efficient. They should be willing to do so if they understand that getting across—the sine qua non of communication—requires a good feeling between people, and efficiency may have to be sacrificed to accomplish human rapport.

9

MASSIVE COMMUNICATION

Mastering one-to-one situations provides relatively good preparation for entering the storm of broader interchange. The veritable blizzard of ongoing transmission in today's society makes it hard enough to get the message, but it's still harder on us if we don't. Whether that message relates to occupational, social, community, or any of countless other subjects, constant communication is being attempted. Abbreviated versions and sophisticated supplements add to the volume. Can't keep up with the books you want to read? You're sure to find a digest or magazine condensation somewhere. Will you miss a discussion on television because you're planning to attend one in person? No problem! You can videotape it automatically from your own set or, lacking equipment, await the rerun. Need the weather forecast, a spiritual inspiration, or even a good joke to start your day? Just dial the appropriate telephone number and it's yours, courtesy of a recording.

Messrs. Bell's and Watson's contributions

The inventor of one of our most wondrous instruments of communication probably had few notions if any of how the telephone might generate confusion or misunderstanding. Nevertheless it has, and as refinements and accessories are added to the basic instrument, the occasions for miscommunication mushroom.

Most of us can duplicate the story of a woman whose son owned a neighborhood butcher shop. Since he also did the buying and delivering, he was frequently out of his store. Thus he missed many incoming phone calls, which meant lost business to him and inconvenience to customers. To solve this problem, he installed one of the new automatic answering machines. However, when his mother was first greeted by her son's recorded voice instructing her to leave a 60-second message after the tone sounded, she proceeded to talk as though he were actually at the other end of the line. Pausing in her comments, she awaited the son's reply, only to be met with complete silence. The woman was distraught, thinking that he had hung up during their conversation, and she asked him about the incident at their next meeting.

The son did his best to explain what had actually happened, drawing an analogy between a mechanical man and the answering device. It would be helpful, he pointed out, if she would begin to accept this new system. "But how will I know if it's the real you that's answering?" inquired the mother. "Easy," he replied. "The recorder won't answer your questions." So as soon as the connection was made on her next call, the mother cleared the air by asking, "Bernie, is that you or the dummy?"

Unlike the butcher's mother, many people in a variety of professions have mastered the art of effective telephone communication. Familiar examples are those who make their living selling by phone, providing information to callers, or accepting orders or bookings. Airline reservation agents are particularly able and efficient phone users, accommodating traveler's needs with a courtesy and poise that each of us could emulate profitably in our own telephone communications.

Although most of us realize that our voices alone must do the communicating in a phone conversation, some still find it difficult to establish rapport with the invisible second party because the nonverbal aspects of the exchange are totally absent. It is true that a smile can be conveyed by the tone of the voice, but it's also a fact that unspoken emotion cannot be transmitted. And while good listening habits are as desirable on the phone as they are in person, lengthy silences can make the speaker wonder whether the receiver is merely concentrating effectively or has fainted.

If we grant the assumption (a safe one, I think) that the majority of us would prefer to see rather than only hear our partner in an exchange, it is interesting to note the public's loss of interest in Picturephones, the devices that bring you the other person's image while you talk. According to a recent newspaper item, most of the initial subscribers have dropped out. Although AT&T issued no detailed report on the explanations given for these withdrawals, it seems that nobody wanted to see the other person in the first place. Why? Did users view the Picturephone as an invasion of privacy or fear that it would invite unexpected and unwelcome intrusions? Could some have felt that the instrument affected communication in an undesirable way?

After all, if people know they're being seen as well as heard, they will be more self-conscious and may adopt distortions of facial expressions and manner—a smile-for-the-camera reaction. Artificiality of this kind would impede rather than enhance communication. Yet somehow, I still think that there are Picturephones in our future and that the subscriber cancellations merely mean a postponement of this tool for effective face-to-face interaction via the wire.

Contrary to the Picturephone's lack of success, most of the technological advances connected with the telephone have been widely and cordially accepted for the same reason that the basic instrument has: convenience and rapidity in communicating. Despite these advantages, it may not be the most effective medium of transmission. In addition to the nonverbal aspects of face-to-face exchanges, telephone calls lack directness and reality. Thus we need to bear in mind that the entire burden of getting our message across rests on the voice alone. As senders, we must enunciate distinctly, speak animatedly, and get to the point. As receivers we must listen attentively but signal our presence occasionally with comments such as "I see" and "Yes." It's also desirable to close a phone conversation with a recap of the conclusions reached or arrangements made if the call involves business or social plans.

Closing a conversation presumes that it gets opened in the first place. It often doesn't. There are large organizations that install direct-dial machinery but forgo the equipment allowing the now-skeletal switchboard staff to switch an incoming call to the new number. If the operators are overburdened, or when they don't really know who is

who, a caller can get caught in a swinging door of tele-
phonic misdirection from operator to wrong line back to
operator and on to another wrong line. The wear and tear
on fingers and patience (to say nothing of the phone bill)
can be considerable.

Then, too, there's always the frustration of not finding
the intended receiver there when you do get the right
number. A friend of mine once spent an unproductive
week trying to telephone an inaccessible (then out-of-
town) colleague who lived at the other end of the city to
ask if he could drop a paper off for signature. Finally my
friend just delivered the document to the peripatetic's
home, where his wife had it signed that night. So the hare
does not always beat the tortoise in communication, and
the desirable medium is the one that gets the message
through best in a particular situation.

One other medium of transmission may be gaining
popularity even faster than the telephone did in its early
years—the computer. Our magazine and newspaper mailing
lists are computerized. So is much of the typesetting of
their printed contents. So are solicitations for charitable
contributions, weather analyses, license plates, consumer
research findings, and most of the control data behind
space travel. But perhaps nowhere is the computer used
with more enthusiasm and abandon than in the business
community.

The most active two-way communication in business
organizations today is not between management and employees but between management and computers. Despite
the user's awareness that the output produced is only as
valid as the input provided, fascination with the electronic

monster continues to increase, pervading the economic as well as the government and social spheres. There are now some observers who await that day when machines will take over the world. The computer already provides strategy alternatives, so why not have it make decisions based on them? A few years ago, data-processing people had to sell management on the computer's potential. Now some of these same people are sounding the alert against the monster's limitations and dangers. A recent cartoon in a financial newspaper showed two people standing alongside a computer, one reading the printout to the other. The caption said, "It's demanding human sacrifice."

Levity aside, there is a menace that is already upon us: the data explosion. Nonsense and garbage proliferate at a highly wasteful rate. Countless little-used or useless reports and statistics get produced by businesses across the country, constituting a type of a scatter-shot communication that is never consummated. When an employee tripped and fell on some stacks of discarded machine reports put into a hallway for rubbish collection, one organization promptly began an analysis of its paper proliferation. The result was a one-third reduction of the data it had been distributing.

Unfortunately most computer users continue to follow the prevailing opposite trend, and their delight in the costly toy at their disposal leads them into a variety of abuses. Many executives engage in communication overkill, deluging the receivers with data in their message. This habit is counterproductive because it drowns the core of the transmission in a sea of information, much of which may have little relevance or lend only marginal support to the sender's objective. Or excessive statistics may be used to create a smoke screen blinding the receiver to something the sender doesn't want explored. In this connection, statistics are like bikinis—what they reveal is interesting, but what they conceal is vital.

Collective communication

Despite the abuses of the telephone and the computer, these and other technologically advanced instruments do vastly enlarge the communicative capacities of people who handle them discriminately. And the computer and the audiovisual media make it possible for hitherto unserviceably large groups to exchange information as units, adding a dimension to human relations that can be exploited for international and generational welfare. A current and tragic example of our failure to function on that plane is the world food crisis, which could have been averted had enough countries responded to information being disseminated by United Nations bodies as early as the latter 1960s.

Thus as we enter the last quarter of this century, the need for exchange within and through groups is rapidly intensifying in direct consequence to the increasing interdependence of ever-larger societal entities. It is not unreasonable to forecast that this need will summon more and more individuals into the role of public communicator, people whose largest audience today may be the participants in a local club meeting or the guests at a wedding reception. Yet these settings provide valuable training for such a role and bear some examining here.

In New England, where my family and I now live, the town meeting is an exercise in group communication as well as democratic government. At one held several years ago, a committee that had been formed to study the acqui-

Just between you and me, Mr. Chairman, members
of the committee, distinguished guests, and untold millions
in the television audience. . . .

sition of land for a new elementary school recommended the purchase of a certain location. The proponents argued that the site would be more expensive later and might even be unavailable. Speakers opposed to the recommendation emphasized the increase in everyone's property taxes that buying the property and eventually constructing the school would entail. For more than an hour, debate centered on financial considerations. Then an unheard-from opponent to the purchase was recognized by the moderator, and, as the saying goes, he showed he had done his homework.

With a battery of statistics to substantiate his comments, the speaker proceeded to explain that the real consideration was lack of need, not the cost factor. Citing a declining birth rate, he argued that classroom space requirements had already stabilized and indeed would begin to contract the following year. The town meeting tabled the land purchase proposal and a subsequent session voted it down. The passage of time confirmed that a new school was in fact unnecessary.

This opposition speaker exemplifies truly effective communication within a group. He clarified thinking, altered perspective, influenced decision making, and saved money. While it's true that timing, crowd emotion, and adherence to the Boy Scout motto all played some part in the outcome, the speaker's skill in stating his message was the principal force that decided the issue.

Interchange with large numbers of people entails subtler and more complex dynamics than does communication among a few. Observe a PTA meeting considering a broad-based field-trip program for elementary school children. Those favoring it stress the educational benefits to the pupils. Opponents counteract that point by stressing the hazards of frequent travel on crowded highways but in fact are concerned with the cost of the program and its impact on the school budget. Although sophisticated communicators sometimes exercise such obfuscation in one-to-one transmissions, it is a far commoner practice in intra-group exchanges.

Group communication incorporates more irrelevance than is ordinarily tolerated in limited encounters. Extraneous remarks give the members of the group the time to digest pertinent information. In this connection, I'm reminded of a meeting of volunteers who had assembled to discuss ways of improving the quality of life in their suburban community. "Will you please stay on the subject?" asked the chairman of the rather large group to admonish a speaker during the warm-up period. "Gladly," replied the offender, "if you'll tell me what the hell it is."

Occasionally the group communication process is reversed, and a large number become the original sender to an individual receiver. A common example of this is the treatment accorded a celebrated personality who appears before or merely visits with a group. All transmissions to this person are tailored to express recognition of his station in life.

This was dramatically demonstrated for me in my previously mentioned summer work at a resort hotel. It was my third season of employment there, and I had progressed from dining room busboy to night club cocktail waiter. One Saturday afternoon, the headliner in that evening's stage show stopped one of us who were working to set up the night club and asked for a rye and soda. The accommodating waiter returned with the drink quickly and served it to the celebrity graciously. However, one gesture was to mar this otherwise flawless performance: on the tray alongside the glass was a check, and he routinely presented it with the drink. The performer was unconcerned; he signed his name and room number to the tab, included a tip, and thanked his server. But when word of this reached the resort owner, he hit the ceiling. How dare the waiter charge for a single drink as though the celebrity were an unknown customer who couldn't be trusted? The waiter obviously hadn't learned that although all men are created equal, eventually some are treated differently.

From groups to masses

Mass interchange serves many purposes. It fills the basic role of stating or answering the thoughts and emotions of a given population. The strength of this expression is relative to the size, credibility, and influence of the group; the transmission can influence opinion, generate legislation, or depose a president. Eventually a group may become large enough to require a spokesman, thus completing the cycle by returning to individual sending through the surrogate who serves as the group's voice.

Sometimes we witness the rise of a self-designated spokesman. This is the case with Ralph Nader, who has emerged as representative for consumers. The amorphous nature of this group and the fact that Nader lacks official endorsement do not lessen his effectiveness. His role has strength because it has the acceptance and support of those being represented. Although such a function had never been recognized before he came along, it was obviously one that begged for implementation.

Public communication, like group exchange, has special characteristics, the most salient of which is that feedback and subsequent response from the sender are either markedly delayed or wholly absent. The very term *communication* and its derivatives do not in fact apply to many settings and actions that they are used to describe. A motion picture company now includes this word in its official name but is of course merely dispensing entertainment. Dozens of companies and other organizations use the term as part of a title for a job that actually involves public relations or employee relations. Radio and television are referred to as electronic communication though what they actually do is send their audiences messages. To be sure, there are countless and subtle types of feedback to mass communications, such as television ratings, reader surveys, and movie attendance records, and these considerations do ultimately affect the output. But they do not really influence the next transmission or perhaps even much later messages.

Although our electronic mass media now permit broadcasting to millions, many people, misled by the carefully cultivated informality of most programs, receive them in much the same vein as they do one-to-one interchanges. This ignores the basic communication link described throughout the preceding chapters. The millions merely become the total of all individual recipients.

Not all (perhaps not even any two) receivers respond to the same message in identical fashion, of course. In training sessions, I used to aim at a "representative segment," feeling that a presentation effective with this smaller group would be beneficial to the whole. In retrospect, I think this was a misconception, since everyone in a group retains individuality and therefore processes the incoming information differently. This would also explain why one-to-one training is fastest and the rate of learning decreases as the size of the group expands.

Nevertheless, it is still the sender's impact on each receiver that determines the effectiveness of mass communication. For example, the success of a public speaker is the result of his acceptance by most of the audience. Now his message may have been received well for different reasons by each, but the end result is positive. While it's true that there is such a thing as a crowd personality, the communication process that fuels this identity stems from the basic one-to-one sender-receiver relationship. Thus the popular entertainer, the public speaker, and the revered novelist alike do not win an audience; they succeed in effectively transmitting their message to most of the individuals in it— a multiplication of one-to-one.

This does not mean that a public communicator cannot discern common attitudes or preferences among the many receivers; on the contrary, a successful mass transmission is proof that he has. I am reminded of an ad for salesmen that I read in my youth and that must have exercised strong pull, because it appeared only once in our local newspaper. It went something like this: "Wanted—brave souls for dangerous journey. Long, dark road to destination; safe return doubtful. Great rewards to those who succeed." Although I never knew how successful this ad was, I did follow up on a classified placed by a frozen food company in a Toronto newspaper many years later. It read: "Uneducated, unmotivated persons needed for poorly paid position. Miserable supervisor, poor working conditions. If not interested, call for appointment." This ad drew an exceptionally large number of replies.

Which demonstrates two things: The public has a funny bone, and if you hit it or any other human response mechanism, you will get your message through.

10

FORWARD TO CLARITY

On December 20, 1972, ten persons died and sixteen others were injured in a two-plane accident at Chicago's O'Hare Airport because the air-traffic controller skipped a word. When the controller told a North Central pilot to use runway 32 for takeoff, he neglected to specify 32 *right* or 32 *left*. A tragic misunderstanding led a Delta pilot to taxi across that same runway. Postcollision safety investigators blamed incomplete communication for the crash. Without understanding the reasons for the existence of two runways with the same number, it could be wondered whether that wasn't the first mistake.

Although poor communication doesn't often have such disastrous consequences as this, the discussion throughout this book has emphasized that it invariably creates some degree of difficulty. Despite my attempt to treat these shortcomings with levity, the fallout from ineffective sending and receiving is frequently of sizable magnitude. It there-

fore appears desirable to suggest some ways we can improve communication throughout society.

Education for communication

A logical starting place for such an ambitious undertaking
would be the classroom. Elementary school is the appropriate level for early training in the basics of getting across
to others and understanding incoming transmissions. It is
axiomatic that what we learn in our young years is not only
immediately but permanently at our command. Teaching
units based on the rudimentary guidelines in Chapter 1
would set the stage for continuing development throughout a child's schooling. Classroom games and role playing
could be used to dramatize the myriad possibilities for misinterpretation and misunderstanding. Awards might be
given to outstanding pupils, and scholastic publications
might feature contests, puzzles, and articles all dedicated
to the improvement of communication.

At the same time that youngsters are learning the
metric system in arithmetic classes, they could be replacing
words and altering contemporary expressions in communications classes. Terms that are out of date, vague, or misleading in meaning could be introduced in the various con-
texts that indicate their definitions or be replaced by more
appropriate terms. The 1974 streaking fad, for example,
begs alteration of the phrase *indecent exposure;* possibly
something like *unwelcome display* might fit contemporary
morality better. In the same year, political events so de-
based the language that much previously understood vocabulary became ambiguous. How do we now interpret
executive privilege? National security gave license to en-

croachments on individual privacy, and *loyalty* meant no holds barred. The same class must also learn to think of the word *executive* as neuter or attach an appropriate gender modifier.

Euphemisms, which proliferated in the 1960s, should give way to concrete expressions. The *senior citizens* and *underprivileged residents* ought once again to be known as the *aged* and as *poor people*. Communication with these groups will be the better for the honesty.

Of course, one of the basic benefits from such early training will be an increased sensitivity to the perspective of a communication partner. Empathy doesn't come easily in today's interchanges, but it can be stimulated. There's the story of a jazz musician who made one of his rare appearances at church on Sunday. After the service, he complimented the minister. "You really flipped me, man," he said. "That was a groovy sermon."

"I'm happy it pleased you," replied the dignified pastor, "but I would appreciate your expressing approval in less vulgar terms."

"Sorry, Daddy," said the jazzman, "but that's my way. I dug your sermon so much I flipped a C-note in the pot."

To which the minister replied, "Cool, man!"

As our growing communicator enters high school, the exercises should become more sophisticated. Training at this level would aim to deepen awareness of the possible outcomes of attempts to exchange information. If people reaching the age of responsibility are conditioned to think along these lines in connection with their transmission and receipt of words, it could also affect their consideration of other acts as well. It has always seemed to me that we give far too little reflection to our actions before we take them.

Some highly productive fallout in the form of a heightened ability to weigh consequences and potential problems in advance of acting could result from early communication training. In this connection, I'm reminded of the newspaper account of a man who put a loaded pistol to his wife's head to "scare her into taking better care of their children." The gun went off. If we grant that the tragic outcome was unpremeditated, it is a ghastly instance of intended communication failing—fatally.

For those who continue their education beyond high school, college curricula could be expanded to include specialized courses on communication pertaining to each field of study. Education majors would become experts at communicating with the age group they were being trained to teach. Student nurses would learn to reach the sick effectively and be receptive to incoming signals from them. Engineering students would receive training in sensitivity to both subordinates and nontechnical personnel for their future success. And so on. Graduate education could extend this empathy even further. A bedside manner would no longer be the special skill of a few gifted physicians. An attorney's legal erudition would be matched by alertness to clients' anxieties as well as to peripheral considerations in a case. This ability would find even broader application if said lawyer were elected to public office or appointed to the bench.

To maintain proficiency, clubs devoted to examining, discussing, and improving interpersonal communication will attract a dedicated membership. Like many organizations currently in existence to build a particular skill, these groups will be of great value to their members. But unlike most such organizations, communication clubs will also provide benefits to society as a whole. The increasing interest in reading and lectures on this subject that is already evident will intensify. Unified local efforts may even produce a national organization, which will further enhance the trend toward making ourselves and our intentions understood.

Many business organizations today offer their managers training in communication. However, unless the participants are new employees they already supervise people and are regularly afforded the opportunity of fouling things up through poor communication habits. In very few cases does a supervisor's communicative ability match his specialized knowledge, and yet his success is probably more closely tied to the former. Future training in effective communication for business managers should focus on advanced levels of the art, with basics already acquired prior to or at the outset of employment.

A universal visual language

Just as laughter and music have long been recognized as languages common to all people, so certain symbols have become internationally understood. On airplanes, the picture of seat belts that lights up is one example. The little outline of a windshield wiper or headlight beam on a dashboard knob of foreign cars is another. Such symbols have been increasing in use and acceptance wherever people who speak different languages convene. This type of communication reaches the intended recipient free of distortion or misleading cues. The drawing of a lighted cigarette broken in half conveys the "No smoking" message in any land. On highways too, signs are beginning to appear with pictures

instead of words indicating that fuel, food, and other serv-
ices are available at a given exit.

One of my first experiences that impressed me with the
need for a standardized visual language occurred in Mexico,
which I visited with an Air Force friend during the mid-
1950s. On the return drive from Monterrey, we ran out of
gas. After succeeding in getting a passing car to stop, we
had to convey our predicament. My high school Spanish
wasn't up to the challenge, so a combination of sign language and improvised symbols had to do the job. It wasn't
difficult to indicate that we were out of fuel. We did this
by pointing to the gas tank, shaking our heads from side
to side, and saying "No" (which fortunately is close to the
negative in all Romance languages). The barriers came
between us after I got into the car with this benefactor to
go for gas. He started to converse with me in his tongue
and I answered in mine, with neither of us understanding
what the other was saying. Several miles later, we arrived
at the first gas station on that two-lane road, and from here
on, the going was smooth. My good Samaritan explained
my plight to the station operator, who in turn sold me a
can of gas and flagged a ride back to my car for me.

It wasn't until I finally arrived there that the success of
this indirect communication began to penetrate. If nothing
else, our experience answered the perennial question: Can
two boys from the States stranded in a foreign country
make their way back to safety without speaking the local
lingo? The answer was yes, but largely because the Mexi-
cans who helped us were masters of both empathy and
nonverbal communication.

In situations like ours, tourists of the future could use
symbol booklets, wallet-size "dictionaries" containing uni-

versally understood drawings representing a variety of predicaments. The traveler in trouble would merely need to locate the appropriate symbol in his booklet and show it to the nearest native, who could reply by pointing to another symbol in the booklet. When one uses a foreign language lexicon, it's still necessary to pronounce each word properly enough to be understood—no easy matter when the language contains sounds English doesn't have, such as the tongue clicks of certain African dialects, or distinctions in intonations that define a word as in Man-

Do you read me, Murdock?   *Yes, loud and clear, Ms. Allen!*

darin Chinese. Symbols would be at once instantly recognizable and clearly interpreted.

I'm reminded again of the visit to Canada I referred to in Chapter 8. On a beautiful drive from Montreal to Quebec, we stopped in another out-of-the-way restaurant, and here only French was spoken. My wife ordered a coffee ice cream cone by requesting "Café glacé." Shortly a glass of iced coffee was placed in front of her, which she promptly consumed rather than risk compounding the confusion. How simple it would have been to point to an entry in a symbol booklet showing an ice-cream cone and then to a subentry picturing a cup of coffee. If such a visual dictionary were available, its symbols would help foreigners everywhere break through barriers of language, educational limitations, and interpretational errors to bring the crystallization usually associated with hindsight to the fore.

Getting across through teamwork

Everything from basketball to sex yields more satisfaction if the people involved are unified in their purposes and procedures. Future communication need be no exception for those who develop expertise in the art now. Moreover the acquisition of the skills associated with it will provide benefits in many other areas as well. Studies, for example, have compared children's IQ scores with their ability to listen attentively and found a high correlation between these powers. The patient receiver who permits a sender to finish transmission without interruption not only gets the completed message but bestows a sense of self-confidence on that communicator. Audience members who judge a speaker on the content of the message rather than on looks, dress, or even manner of delivery will not only be honest with that sender but avoid the distortions caused by prejudice.

Two of the best communicators I know achieve effectiveness because they have the ability to make full partners of the other person or people in a conversation. One is Professor Walter Salmon, of the Harvard Business School, and the other is Malcolm Sherman, a retailing executive. Although each is a rugged individualist and quite different from the other in personality and style of communication, both have the talent to engage themselves wholly in the communication process.

Walter Salmon has developed a superb questioning technique that subtly penetrates to the core of a subject. In using it, he in no way stifles his communication partner's spontaneous comments; in fact, his pleasant and casual application of it encourages continuing feedback. It's as though he were functioning in two roles—as a moderator and as a sender-receiver. Capping this talent are a disarming sense of humor and exceptional articulateness.

Mal Sherman's attributes begin with a total absence of pretension. He listens attentively, rarely interrupts, and clarifies points as they evolve. He uses his knowledge of human behavior to understand and adjust to unexpected or unfavorable reactions during an interchange. Finally, his timing is excellent, and he knows just when to break a dialog with humor or move on to another subject.

One of the most impressive specific interchanges I have ever been party to took place during the meeting with Milton Eisenhower that I described briefly in Chapter 5. He engaged me in low-key, informal conversation, making casual and to-the-point remarks that both put me at my ease and conveyed his interest in what I had to say. Already aware of Dr. Eisenhower's forensic powers, I now saw the versatility of his skills in a one-to-one encounter. To this day, his approach remains for me a model of effective discourse. Some people would call it the effect of charisma or charm, but I recall it as the result of true communicative excellence.

There is no set pattern for the effective communicator. Each of us should in fact develop a personal style based on good practices but reflecting our individuality. Some of the guidelines covered in this book might seem self-evident to instinctively fine communicators, but these people are a scarce breed, as are the exceptionally gifted in any human activity. For most of us, the art demands training, practice, and, not least, the frequent self-reminder of who we are, who the other person is, and what the circumstances of our exchange happen to be.

The expert communicator is the neighbor who converses with next-door preschool children without resorting to baby talk, or the teacher who can stimulate pupils during class hours and then converse easily with adults after school. A teenager's parent who shows respect for the youngster's opinions is another example. So is the business manager who transfers gracefully from on-the-job discussions to after-hours social exchanges with subordinates. All these are people who have developed the ability to make their transmissions reflect the role they play and the atmosphere in which it is implemented.

The wrap-up

When we consider the difficulty we routinely encounter in breaking the comprehension barrier, it is puzzling why more people aren't working at getting across. We should approach communicating as we do any act requiring skill, by preparing ourselves. The tools are easy to use and accessible to all.

As senders, we're involved in the more active (and probably more enjoyable) of the two communicative functions. First consideration must be given to the identity of our receiver: What is the relationship of this person to the nature of our message, and what are our respective roles? Then what is the intent behind our communicating? Now we are ready to interact, in verbal or written exchange, so we (1) assume the appropriate role, (2) convey an earnest desire to get our message across, and (3) transmit the information in a plain and straightforward manner. Having sent out our thoughts, we now elicit feedback to insure that our message has been received correctly.

Unsatisfactory feedback necessitates a second effort, during which these same steps are repeated. However, we should first pause a moment to assess which one of us contributed what to our initial failure. In this way, we can sometimes eliminate part of the procedure the second time around and concentrate on the trouble spots.

Then it happens! The sweet success of obtaining total comprehension is ours. The effort underlying the accomplishment seems small indeed compared with the satisfaction and results it brings.

When we act as a receiver, dedication to understanding is paramount. Attentiveness and good listening habits are primary aids. Self-control will harness the natural tendency to interrupt and switch our role to that of sender. Keeping an open mind, which is the most difficult task for most receivers, enables us to receive the whole of the incoming transmission without distorting or rejecting material that conflicts with our predispositions. Finally, we must obtain clarification of anything that we do not understand, and we do this, of course, by questioning the sender. Even things that seem clear should be confirmed. And there it is! That satisfying feeling of getting the message exactly as it was-intended is ours.

The nineteenth-century historian Thomas Carlyle once wrote, "Make yourself an honest man, and then you may be sure that there is one less rascal in the world." To adapt that injunction to the objective of this book, if each of us succeeds in becoming a good communicator, we may be certain that we've contributed to better understanding in our part of the world.

AMACOM Executive Books-Paperbacks

John D. Arnold	The Art of Decision Making: 7 Steps to Achieving More Effective Results	$6.95
Eugene J. Benge	Elements of Modern Management	$5.95
Dudley Bennett	TA and the Manager	$4.95
Warren Bennis	The Unconscious Conspiracy	$4.95
Don Berliner	Want a Job? Get Some Experience...	$5.95
Borst & Montana	Managing Nonprofit Organizations	$5.95
J. Douglas Brown	The Human Nature of Organizations	$3.95
Ronald D. Brown	From Selling to Managing	$4.95
Richard E. Byrd	A Guide to Personal Risk Taking	$4.95
Logan Cheek	Zero-Base Budgeting Comes of Age	$6.95
William A. Cohen	The Executive's Guide to Finding a Superior Job	$5.95
Richard R. Conarroe	Bravely, Bravely in Business	$8.95
Ken Cooper	Bodybusiness	$5.95
James J. Cribbin	Effective Managerial Leadership	$5.95
John D. Drake	Interviewing for Managers	$5.95
Sidney Edlund	There Is a Better Way to Sell	$5.95
Norman L. Enger	Management Standards for Developing Information Systems	$5.95
Figueroa & Winker	A Business Information Guidebook	$9.95
Saul W. Gellerman	Motivation and Productivity	$5.95
Roger A. Golde	Muddling Through	$5.95
Bernard Haldane	Career Satisfaction and Success	$3.95
Lois B. Hart	Moving Up! Women and Leadership	$6.95
Hart & Schleicher	A Conference and Workshop Planner's Manual	$15.95
Michael Hayes	Pay Yourself First: The High Beta/No-Load Way to Stock Market Profits	$6.95
Maurice R. Hecht	What Happens in Management	$7.95
Charles L. Hughes	Goal Setting	$4.95
John W. Humble	How to Manage By Objectives	$5.95
Jones & Trentin	Budgeting (rev. ed.)	$12.95
William H. Krause	How to Hire and Motivate Manufacturer's Representatives	$4.95
Sy Lazarus	A Guide to Effective Communication	$5.95
Philip R. Lund	Compelling Selling	$4.95